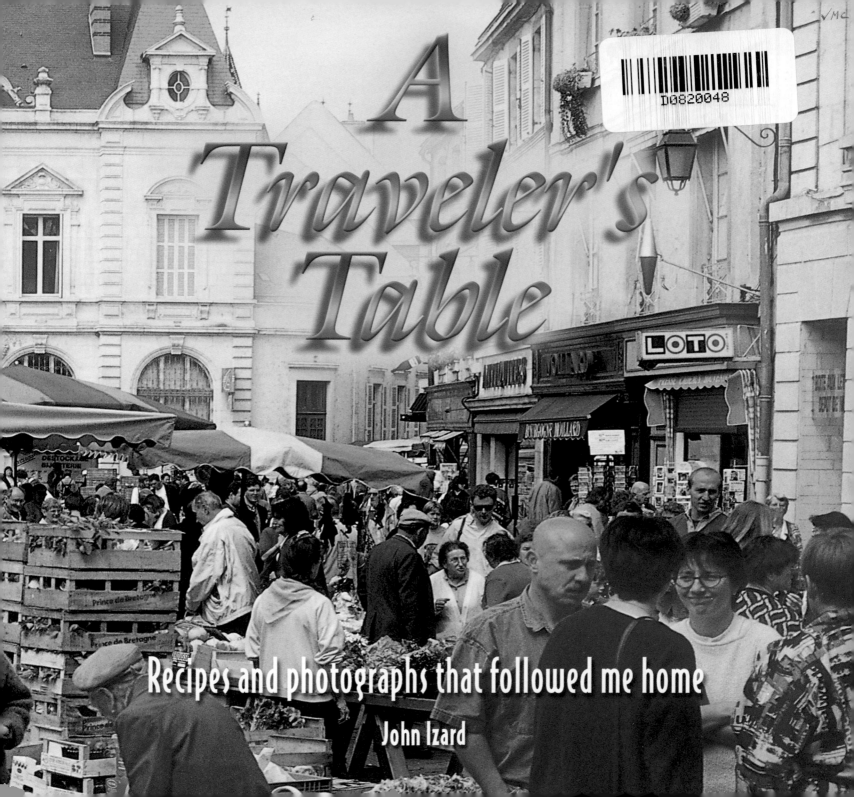

A Traveler's Table

Recipes and photographs that followed me home

John Izard

Cover Photograph: On an Easter morning, between Athens and Delphi, Greece, a shepherd leads his flock homeward.

Inside cover photograph: Along the Rhône River, market day in Viviers, France.

Except for three, all photographs were taken by the author during his travels.

Copyright © 2002

John Izard

ISBN: 0-9723815-0-3

Library of Congress Control Number: 2002115181

First Printing   November   2002

WIMMER
COOKBOOKS

ConsolidatedGraphics

1-800-548-2537

Table of Contents

Introduction

"I would like to try all of your recipes." Comments like this from several people who looked over drafts of my cookbook encouraged me to have it published.

Every niche in the culinary field is covered by one or more of the hundreds of cookbooks currently in print. There hardly seems room for another specialty cookbook. What I have tried to do, therefore, is put together a collection of especially good recipes that meet one of two criteria: either they are (1) quite unusual or (2) the best I ever tasted. Also to be included, I must like the recipe. It is my hope that the user will want to try a lot of these recipes. Some of my favorites are highlighted in the introductions to the sections.

The photographs in this volume represent a happy convergence of two of my hobbies - photography and cooking. I did not set out to take pictures as illustrations for a cookbook. Rather I was a typical tourist trying to record the interesting facets of life in the countries we visited. Over the years, I accumulated something in the order of 7,500 color slides. When my idea of doing a cookbook dawned, I realized that I already had a great many photos dealing with food and cooking. From that point forward, however, I made a greater effort to take pictures that might illustrate a cookbook.

My photographs provide a panorama of food and cooking from many parts of our country as well as many countries around the globe. They are intended to convey an appreciation of the wide world of food.

Back to the recipes, they are not hard to prepare, and I have included detailed instructions in instances where help might be useful. Since I am not a trained chef myself, any home cook should be able to follow my recipes.

On the other hand, I do recommend the best available ingredients and that recipes be prepared with care and attention to detail. This book does not include many shortcuts such as starting with a can of creamed mushroom soup or marinating something in Italian dressing. In my experience, these approaches rarely produce an exceptional dish.

Also, a nice presentation always adds to the appreciation of a meal. Nothing fancy is required. Just put things carefully in appropriate serving dishes or arrange them neatly on plates. Salad plates are well worth the extra trouble. Without them, you will find sauces and salad dressings migrating to unwanted places.

In sum, this collection includes a wide assortment of unusual recipes that are well within the capability of the home cook. I hope that they will provide excitement and variety to your table!

To
Bishop Jefferts Schori

Looking forward
to working together
on "Grow Faith".
I hope that
this book will
add new zest
to your table.

[signature]

October 2006

*The author with an Atlantic salmon,
from Iceland's River Vatnsdals'a*

Acknowledgments

The inspiration for many of my recipes undoubtably came from a chef or home cook. Fading memories as well as the evolution of particular recipes make it impossible for me to trace the origins of most recipes. To each of these sources, however, I express my admiration and thanks.

I can identify a few recipes with the people who shared them with me. I have tried to acknowledge them and express my thanks to one and all.

Marilyn Radovich, a retired secretary from King and Spalding; my secretary, Charlotte Oberto; and Marilyn's sister, Marsha Lester, who is invaluable to me at the office, have each had an important part in compiling this book.

My thanks are extended to Jack Burton, the ex-advertising guru, who was most generous in offering suggestions about content and style.

I also want to thank our children Sadie, John and Bailey – each of them a fine cook. Some of their recipes are included.

The marvelous job done by the personnel at Wimmer Cookbooks is obvious. To them goes credit for the style and technical perfection. Particularly, I express my gratitude to Sheila Thomas, Patty Croft, Jim Davidson, and Maureen Fortune, who led my team at Wimmer.

Finally, I would never have completed this book without constant support and assistance from my wife, Mary. We spent endless hours together working on the text, and she was the source of many helpful ideas. Incidentally, she would rather grow vegetables than cook them.

The author's wife, Mary, in Yellowstone National Park, 1977.

THE EPISCOPAL
MEDIA CENTER

As a Trustee and former Chairman of the Episcopal Media Center, I am donating a portion of the press run of these cookbooks to the Center. It is a national, non-profit organization committed to using the electronic media to bring Christian faith and values to the culture at large. The Center will use these books to encourage support and otherwise help in its endeavors.

Few will disagree that in today's world, electronic media have a huge influence on the public; yet, mainline churches, whose teachings underpin the greatness of our country, are strangely absent from the air waves.

The Episcopal Media Center seeks effective, thoughtful and entertaining ways to utilize the electronic media for the noble purposes that Christianity has fostered for two thousand years. Whether it is through productions of literary works that reinforce the church's message such as "The Chronicles of Narnia" by C.S. Lewis, or through engaging and inviting television spots, or through participation in radio's award-winning Protestant Hour (now televised on The Hallmark Channel as "Day One"), the Episcopal Media Center is breaking new ground.

These programs show what can be done. It is our hope that they will encourage the church to develop a stronger voice in addressing the complex problems and needs that face all of us today.

www.episcopalmedia.org

How to Use This Cookbook

This cookbook is divided into ten sections, the titles of which are largely self-explanatory. Scattered through the text are a number of short discussions of interesting culinary topics. Each discussion is headed "About" (E.g., About Hamburgers, About Oil and Vinegar Dressing and About Onions). Sidebars are small comments that may amplify some aspect of a recipe or contain interesting tangential material.

The locations of recipes for sauces merit mention. Sauces that are special to a particular recipe are listed with that recipe. Sauces intended for more general use are interspersed in the sections where they are most often used. Salad dressings appear with salads.

The Index is comprehensive and should be invaluable to the user. Besides an alphabetical listing for each recipe, recipes are collected under every possible category. Thus the discussions starting "About" are listed under "About." All sauces appear under that heading. Other interesting subheadings include Charcoal Broiling (of which there are about 20 recipes); Pickles, Pickled; and Sandwiches.

Finally, the Index has a geographic section that lists foreign recipes by their country of origin. Sixteen countries are represented.

As for individual recipes, ingredients are listed and directions given in standard form. The proper identification of some common ingredients as well as the exact meaning of some terms should be helpful. This information follows in alphabetical order.

Chopping. This cookbook refers to 3 sizes of chopped ingredients: finely chopped, chopped and coarsely chopped. Diced is also used and suggests that ingredients be cut in more even shapes (a dimension is generally given). Minced means to chop as finely as possible.

Flour. All-purpose flour unless otherwise stated.

Seasoned flour. When mentioned in recipes, means all-purpose flour seasoned with salt and regular ground black pepper. To a cup of flour add about ½ teaspoon salt and ¼ teaspoon black pepper, or more, to taste.

Hot sauce. Tabasco is the best known and has a wide following. Crystal, Louisiana, Red Rooster and other common hot sauces are not quite as hot and add more pepper flavor; I generally use them. If you use Tabasco, reduce the amounts specified in these recipes by one third.

Measures. Level unless otherwise stated.

Milk and cream. Labels on milk and cream can be confusing. The significant difference between the various products is the butter fat content. Current labeling practices are:

Product	Butter Fat Content
skim milk	0
1% milk	1%
2% milk	2%
whole milk	3%
cream (coffee cream)	4%
half-and-half	5%
whipping cream	7%
heavy whipping cream	8%

In this book, milk means whole milk, and cream means coffee cream. *Heavy whipping cream* may be substituted for whipping cream for a particularly rich dish.

Olive oil. Extra virgin every time. Depending on your taste and the particular recipe, you may use a full-bodied oil or one with a more subtle flavor.

Paprika. Sweet Hungarian Paprika imparts more flavor than the ordinary variety, and I generally prefer it, particularly in dishes where paprika is the dominate flavor. E.g., Quail Paprika, p.135.

Parsley. Modern chefs believe that flat leaf (Italian) parsley imparts more flavor than the ordinary variety. The latter when shredded, however, gives a crinkley texture which I believe is more important than a slight variation in flavor.

Red pepper and *cayenne* are interchangeable.

Spices. References are to dried herbs unless otherwise noted. As a general rule, use twice as much fresh herb as its dried counterpart.

Temperatures are given in degrees Fahrenheit. Oven temperature gauges vary somewhat, and you may need to make adjustments based on your particular oven.

Worcestershire sauce. Always Lea & Perrins.

Once again, I call your attention to the copious index. It should point the way to answers to any other questions that arise.

Appetizers

*Market day in a
Peruvian village square.*

Appetizers

In modern times various small plates and snacks have been served before or at the beginning of a meal and referred to as Appetizers or Hors D'oeuvre. The latter is French for "outside the work" or outside the main meal.

In common usage, "hors d'oeuvre" is more often used to refer to snacks, chips and other items served during the cocktail hour. As such, they are not really part of the meal, but may dispense with the need for an appetizer.

Hors d'oeuvre, or "Hors d'oeuvres" in the Americanized version, can be hot or cold. Historically the term referred to a mini buffet which might include smoked fish, eggs, pickled vegetables, salads and the like. The diner made a selection from this panoply as a first course. This type of presentation remains common in many European countries today.

At home an appetizer tends to be a more specialized offering typified by the ubiquitous shrimp cocktail. More unusual cold appetizers are Avocado Cocktail, p.13, Eggs à la Russe, p.18, and Game Bird Terrine, p.30. On the hot side, excellent choices are Mushrooms Flambé, p.19, and Grilled Vidalia Onion Appetizer, p.24.

Appetizers tend to merge with salads and soups which often take their place on a menu.

Avocado Cocktail

1   large avocado, cut into ½ inch dice

1-2   ripe tomatoes, cut into ¼ inch dice

4   tablespoons finely chopped onion

4   tablespoons dill pickle relish

Lettuce leaves

Lemon wedges for garnish

You should have about twice as much avocado as tomato.

Toss avocado, tomatoes, onion and relish to mix.

Dressing

3   tablespoons olive oil

4   tablespoons lemon juice

3   tablespoons chili sauce

½   teaspoon salt

⅛   teaspoon black pepper

Mix dressing, pour over avocado mixture and toss lightly. Chill well and serve on lettuce leaves with lemon wedges.

Serves 4.

Black Bean and Raspberry Salsa Dip

1   (15 ounce) can black beans

½   cup finely chopped onion

8   ounces cream cheese, softened

1   cup hot tomato salsa

⅓   cup seedless raspberry preserves

1   teaspoon chili powder

½   cup Monterey Jack and/or Colby cheese, coarsely grated

Drain the black beans and mash with a fork. Mix well with onion and cream cheese. Spread the bean mixture in the bottom of a 1½ inch deep pie dish. Mix the tomato salsa and raspberry preserves. Spread over the bean mixture and sprinkle with chili powder. Top with the grated cheese. Put the pie dish, uncovered, in a preheated 350 degree oven and bake for 30 minutes. Let cool slightly and serve as a dip with a combination of salsa chips and crackers.

Cheese Biscuits

(Margaret Whittemore's Aunt Lib)

The Rice Krispies make this recipe stand out from conventional recipes for cheese biscuits.

1 stick butter (salted)	1 cup flour (scant)
1 cup sharp Cheddar cheese, grated and slightly packed	⅛-¼ teaspoon cayenne pepper, to taste
	1 cup Rice Krispies

Cut butter in slices and bring to room temperature. In an electric beater, mix butter, cheese, flour and cayenne. When well creamed, add Rice Krispies and continue mixing until well blended.

Roll dough into 1½ inch logs and cut into ¼ inch slices. Put slices on a cookie sheet and bake in the center of a preheated 350 degree oven for 15 to 20 minutes until nice and crisp. Biscuits do not do well with more than one pan in the oven.

Biscuits will keep in a sealed can for 2 weeks or so and can be crisped in the oven if necessary.

Cream Cheese and Olive Sandwich

1 small package cream cheese	Thin slices white bread (crusts removed)
½ cup finely chopped pimento stuffed green olives	

Mix cream cheese and olives. Spread on one bread slice and top with another. In toaster oven or broiler, toast sandwiches until bread is nicely browned on both sides. Cut sandwiches in halves or thirds and serve while still warm.

Cheerful lady tending cheese booth at a small town market, Ireland.

Cheese Squares

(Tybee Island, Georgia)

1	loaf white bread	½	teaspoon mild curry powder
1	stick butter, at room temperature	¼	teaspoon salt
½	teaspoon garlic salt		

Remove crusts from loaf of bread. Slice very thin (special devices to slice regular slices of bread in half are available in cookware stores). Blend butter, garlic salt, curry powder and salt.

Stack 3 slices of bread "buttered" with the butter mixture between slices. Cut each stack into 9 cubes.

"Icing"

2	glasses Old English cheese spread (5 ounces each)	2	tablespoons Worcestershire sauce
1½	sticks butter, at room temperature	½	teaspoon salt
1	egg, beaten	¼	teaspoon cayenne pepper

Blend cheese spread and butter. Mix in egg, Worcestershire sauce, salt and cayenne. With this mixture, "ice" each cube on all sides except the bottom. Store cubes in freezer until ready to use.

Remove cubes from the freezer and bake unthawed in a preheated 400 degree oven until slightly firm (15 to 20 minutes). If not lightly brown on top, run under the broiler for a couple of minutes. Serve while still hot.

Serves 20 to 25.

Mandarin Chicken Bites

2	whole chicken breasts, about 2 pounds	1	pound spinach leaves, rinsed and stemmed
1¾	cups chicken broth	2	quarts boiling water
¼	cup soy sauce	2	cans Mandarin orange sections, drained (16 ounce)
1	tablespoon Worcestershire sauce		

In a saucepan, combine chicken breasts, broth, soy sauce and Worcestershire sauce. Bring to boil and simmer covered until chicken is fork tender (about 15 to 20 minutes). With a slotted spoon, remove chicken from broth and let cool slightly. Remove and discard skin and bones. Cut chicken into 1 inch cubes.

Place spinach leaves in a colander. Pour boiling water over leaves. Drain and set aside to cool.

Place a cube of chicken at stem end of a spinach leaf and wrap leaf over chicken so that chicken still shows on sides. Secure leaf with a wooden pick. Refrigerate at least 1 hour. Recipe can be prepared up to this point a day or two ahead.

To serve, add one Mandarin orange section at the end of each wooden pick. Serve with Curry Mayonnaise Dip.

Curry Mayonnaise Dip

¼	cup mayonnaise	2	tablespoons finely chopped Indian chutney
¼	cup sour cream		
2	teaspoons medium curry powder		

Blend foregoing ingredients.

Serves 8.

Curry-Dill Dip
(For Raw Vegetables)

1 cup sour cream	2 tablespoons chopped fresh parsley or 1 tablespoon dried parsley
1 cup mayonnaise	2 teaspoons mild curry powder
1 tablespoon finely chopped chives or onion	2 teaspoons dill weed
	1 teaspoon seasoned salt (E.g., Jane's Krazy)

Mix all ingredients and let stand at least 24 hours in the refrigerator. Use as dip for raw celery, carrots, green onions, cucumbers, radishes, kohlrabi, cauliflower, turnips; or as a topping for hot green vegetables.

An unusually tasty dip that originated outside Savannah in Vernonburg, Georgia.

Golden Cocktail Balls

2 cups sharp Cheddar cheese, grated	¼ teaspoon dry mustard
½ cup margarine, softened	1 teaspoon paprika
1 cup flour	48 pimento stuffed, small green olives

With an electric mixer, cream cheese and margarine. Add flour, mustard and paprika and mix well – may have to mix with hands as mixture will be thick. Drain olives well and dry on paper towels. Take about ⅙ of the dough at a time and with your hands roll dough into a cylinder about ½ inch in diameter. Pinch off approximately ½ inch sections of dough and roll into balls the size of a large marble. With a ball in palms of your hands flatten to ⅛ inch thickness. Place an olive in the center and roll up and seal the olive. You may need a little flour on your hands to keep dough from sticking.

Place cheese balls on an ungreased baking sheet and bake in a preheated 400 degree oven for 10 to 12 minutes (until cheese balls are firm and slightly browned). May serve cheese balls hot or save for several days in the refrigerator and serve at room temperature.

Deviled Eggs

6	eggs	¼	teaspoon salt
2½	tablespoons mayonnaise		Paprika for garnish
1½	teaspoons prepared mustard		Parsley for garnish
½	teaspoon dry mustard		

Hard-boil and peel eggs. Slice in half lengthwise. Remove yolks and put in a small bowl. Mash yolks with a fork. Add mayonnaise, prepared mustard, dry mustard and salt. Mix well. Heap yolk mixture back into egg halves. Top each egg with a dash of paprika and a parsley sprig.

Serves 8.

Eggs à la Russe

8	slices white bread	2	tablespoons lemon juice
1	tube anchovy paste		Olive oil
8	hard-boiled eggs, peeled	2-3	firm ripe tomatoes, cut in 8 – ¼ inch slices
1	cup mayonnaise (preferably homemade)		
2	ounces small caviar (preferably red)	8	lettuce leaves

Using a plastic or other round glass, cut 1 circular piece (about 3 inches in diameter) from each slice of bread. Toast bread rounds in a slow oven until they are just crisp. Cut a horizontal slice off the thick end of each egg so that the egg will stand up. Mix the mayonnaise and caviar and then mix in the lemon juice and enough olive oil to make the mayonnaise drip off the edge of a spoon.

Spread one side of each toast round with anchovy paste, top with a slice of tomato and set an egg on the tomato. Spoon 2 to 3 tablespoons of the mayonnaise mixture over each egg and let the mayonnaise run down the sides of the egg. Arrange lettuce leaves on individual salad plates and put 1 egg ensemble on each.

Serves 8.

Pickled Eggs

12	eggs	1½	teaspoons mustard seed
3	cups cider vinegar	3	bay leaves
1¼	cups water	1	tablespoon whole black peppercorns
½	cup olive oil	2	medium sweet onions, thinly sliced
4	teaspoons salt	4	cloves garlic, thinly sliced
1½	teaspoons celery seed	1	dozen sprigs parsley

Hard-boil eggs by starting eggs in cool water, bringing to a simmer and simmering for 12 to 15 minutes. Plunge hard-cooked eggs in cold water and peel.

Mix vinegar, water and olive oil in a large jar. Add salt, celery seed, mustard seed, bay leaves and peppercorns. Mix. Then add eggs, onions, garlic and parsley so that everything is well combined.

Let eggs stand in refrigerator for at least 1 week to blend flavors. Serve eggs with some of the onion and parsley.

Eggs will keep 2 to 3 weeks or more in the refrigerator.

At the start of World War II, pickled eggs were a standby at the taverns in Northampton, Massachusetts – the seat of Smith College. A big jar stood on every bar and provided the only solid food for many visiting Yale men.

Mushrooms Flambé

½	stick butter		Salt, to taste
1	pound fresh mushrooms, sliced		Ground nutmeg (couple of dashes)
½	cup sherry	4	tablespoons brandy
	Juice of 1 lemon	⅔	cup whipping cream
1	tablespoon Worcestershire sauce	6	thin slices white bread, toasted
	Red pepper, to taste		

Melt butter in a sauté pan and cook mushrooms until lightly browned. Add sherry, lemon juice and Worcestershire sauce and simmer until pan is nearly dry. Add red pepper, salt, nutmeg and brandy. Set pan afire and stir until flames go out. Add cream and stir to combine.

Mushrooms Flambé make a fine hors d'oeuvre served in a chaffing dish with toast triangles. Or the dish may be served on toast as a first course.

Serves 6.

Guacamole

Hucksters at curb markets, fairs and carnivals draw large crowds demonstrating tricky devices that effortlessly slice, peel or shape vegetables. Ordinarily, gullible buyers lack the manual dexterity to duplicate these remarkable feats.

1   large ripe avocado (1½ small)

1   medium ripe tomato, peeled, seeded and chopped medium fine

3   tablespoons finely chopped onion

1   teaspoon minced fresh jalapeño pepper

1   tablespoon coarsely shredded fresh cilantro

¼   teaspoon chili powder (preferably hot)

⅓   teaspoon salt

1½   tablespoons lime juice

1   tablespoon olive oil

Peel avocado, discard seed and cut avocado into ½ inch dice. With a knife and fork cut and mash avocado leaving some texture in the mixture. Mix the avocado, tomato, onion, jalapeño and cilantro. Sprinkle with chili powder and salt. Then pour on lime juice and olive oil. Mix well. Let guacamole stand in refrigerator an hour or longer to blend flavors. Serve with tortilla chips. Saltines or other crackers can be substituted for the chips.

If you do not have an jalapeño, substitute ⅛ teaspoon black pepper. If you do not have cilantro, do not be concerned as the guacamole is very good without it.

An appealing vegetable display, Athens, Greece.

Mushroom Appetizer

(O'Briens in Bozeman)

1	pound mushrooms	½	teaspoon salt
4	tablespoons olive oil	¼	teaspoon black pepper
½	cup coarsely chopped onion	4	tablespoons dry sherry
4	garlic cloves, sliced	⅓	cup dry white wine
¾	teaspoon powdered marjoram	⅓	cup whipping cream
3	dashes nutmeg	6	thin slices white bread, toasted

Separate mushroom caps and stems. Cut caps in thin vertical slices and stems in thin horizontal slices. Heat olive oil in a skillet and sauté onions and garlic until limp. Add mushrooms and continue to sauté until well heated. Add marjoram, nutmeg, salt and pepper; then add sherry and continue cooking for a couple of minutes. Add white wine and simmer until mushrooms are cooked and most of the wine has evaporated. Reduce heat, stir in cream and let thicken. Serve on toast triangles as an appetizer.

Serves 6.

Curb market on the bay, Porte Montt, Chile.

Grilled Portabello Mushrooms

(With Fresh Tomatoes)

8	medium portabello mushrooms	4	tablespoons olive oil
1½	cups ripe tomatoes, seeded and cut into medium dice (Roma tomatoes are a good choice)	1	tablespoon balsamic vinegar
		½	teaspoon salt
2	medium cloves garlic, finely chopped	¼	teaspoon freshly ground black pepper
			Parsley for garnish

Remove stems from mushrooms and reserve for another use. Grill mushroom caps on a hot grill until cooked through. (If a grill is not handy, you can sear mushrooms quickly in a little olive oil in a hot iron skillet.) Cut mushrooms in quarter inch vertical slices.

Put chopped tomatoes, chopped garlic, olive oil, vinegar, salt and pepper in a sauté pan over medium heat and stir until just heated through. Arrange mushroom slices on individual plates and generously top with the tomato mixture. Garnish with fresh parsley.

Serves 6.

Mustard Vinaigrette Dip

⅓	cup tarragon vinegar	3-4	tablespoons fresh herbs (parsley, basil, tarragon, chervil, dill), minced
⅓	cup Dijon type prepared mustard		Salt and black pepper to taste
1	cup olive oil		
1	shallot, minced		

Whisk vinegar and mustard together. Add oil, bit by bit, whisking vigorously (dip should be the consistency of light mayonnaise). Season with shallot, minced herbs and salt and pepper to taste.

Delicious with an assortment of Blanched Vegetables, p.32.

Pickled Olives

44 ounces (about) assorted pitted olives
2   cups olive oil
2   cups red wine vinegar
1   cup liquid from green olives
8   garlic cloves, sliced
2   tablespoons black peppercorns
1   tablespoon crushed red pepper
12 bay leaves
2   teaspoons oregano
2   teaspoons thyme leaves

Rind of 1 lemon, cut in strips
1   bunch parsley
2   medium onions, sliced

Obtain a good selection of olives, green and black, large and small, including some pimento stuffed olives.

In a large jar mix all ingredients together and let stand for a week or so. Stir occasionally. Additional olives may be added to the pickling mixture after the first batch has been used.

The parsley and/or onions may be omitted if you prefer the olives alone. If used, however, serve a little parsley and onion with the olives.

Can make ½ of this recipe.

Olive salesman, Honfleur, France.

Grilled Vidalia Onion Appetizer

3-4	medium Vidalia or other sweet onions	1	cup cream sauce
½	stick butter, melted	½	cup finely chopped red bell pepper
8	slices bacon		Salt and black pepper to taste
8	sprigs watercress		

Peel and cut onions in ⅜ inch horizontal slices (should have 12 slices). Brush onion slices with butter and broil close to the heat source until lightly browned on one side. Cook bacon slices until crisp. On each of 4 small plates put 3 slices of onion in a single layer, topped with 2 slices bacon and 2 sprigs of watercress.

Make a Cream Sauce, p.115, using 1 cup milk. Stir in the red bell pepper. Season sauce with salt and black pepper to taste. Pour a little sauce over the center of each appetizer.

Serves 4.

Vidalia Onion Dip

1	cup Vidalia or other sweet, yellow onion, cut in ¼ inch dice	¾	cup mayonnaise (commercial is preferable to homemade)
1	cup coarsely grated Swiss cheese		

Combine onion, Swiss cheese and mayonnaise. Spread in a pie pan or other shallow baking pan (mixture should be about 1 inch deep). Bake in a preheated 350 degree oven until brown and bubbling (about 1 hour).

Serve dip with wheat thins, pita triangles or triskets.

This dip is particularly appealing in a party chafing dish. It gives off a pleasant aroma and guests think that it is a much more complicated concoction. You may freeze excess dip before baking.

Oyster Cracker Snack

1	box oyster crackers (about 1 quart)	1½	tablespoons dill weed
½	cup corn oil	1	tablespoon lemon-pepper seasoning
⅔	small (1 ounce) package Hidden Valley Original Ranch Dressing (a powder)		

Put crackers in a bowl. Drizzle with oil while stirring crackers. Then mix in Ranch Dressing, dill weed and lemon pepper. Put crackers in a plastic bag and shake to mix well again. Crackers may be kept for a week or so in a sealed tin and may also be frozen.

This recipe is very good with olive oil instead of corn oil.

This snack makes a welcome, small hostess gift.

Port Wine Cheese Spread

(Jean Veach)

1	pound sharp Cheddar cheese	1	tablespoon dry mustard
2	tablespoons Worcestershire sauce	¾	teaspoon salt
4	tablespoons port wine	4	tablespoons milk
1½	tablespoons prepared horseradish		

Mix all ingredients together and refrigerate for several hours before using. Serve with crackers or toast points.

About Smoked Salmon

The term, "Smoked Salmon" covers a wide range of products. To begin with, traditional smoked salmon comes from that great game fish, Atlantic Salmon (Salmo salar). Let's put Pacific salmon in a separate category.

As far as I know, smoked salmon was first exported from Scotland and England. There, fresh sides of salmon are smoked over apple, alder or other wood at low temperatures for a day or longer. Good smoked Atlantic salmon also comes from Norway, Canada and other countries.

Smoked salmon should be sliced very thin and served as an appetizer or used to add its flavor to other dishes. Traditionally, smoked salmon is served with toast points, lemon wedges and side dishes of capers, minced onion and grated hard-boiled egg.

Gravlax is Atlantic salmon cured by a salt process, generally with fresh dill. It bears some resemblance to smoked salmon and is delicious, served with a sweet mustard sauce.

Pacific smoked salmon comes from the various species of west coast salmon and is ordinarily smoked by a hot process and frequently canned. The smoked salmon recipes in this cookbook are not intended for west coast salmon.

Before "Catch and release"; cutthroat trout, Grand Canyon of the Yellowstone.

Brie Cheese with Smoked Salmon and Dill

Brie cheese
Smoked Atlantic salmon, thinly sliced
  and coarsely chopped

Fresh dill, coarsely chopped

For this recipe, you may use a whole round of Brie cheese or if you want a smaller quantity, use a triangular section of the cheese. In either case, slice the cheese in half horizontally. On the bottom slice of the Brie spread a ¼ inch layer of chopped salmon and cover generously with chopped dill. Top with the other slice of cheese. Spread another layer of chopped salmon on top of the Brie and cover the Brie and the outside of the cheese with chopped dill.

Serve the cheese with a selection of crackers as an hors d'oeuvre.

Smoked Whitefish Dip

2-3 medium-size smoked whitefish
1   pint sour cream

1   small package cream cheese, softened
Juice of 1 lemon

Whitefish are generally sliced in half before smoking. If whole, however, slice the fish in half along the backbone. Flake meat from skin. Mix sour cream, cream cheese and lemon juice. Then mix in flaked white fish and chill.

Serve the dip on crackers.

To the dip, you may add Worcestershire sauce and/or hot sauce to taste.

Smoked Whitefish

Whitefish are native in the rivers of the American Northwest. Fish 13 to 15 inches long are ideal for smoking.

Clean fish, remove heads and soak overnight in a mixture of:

2	quarts water	1	cup salt
1	cup dark brown sugar		

The next day, split fish in half and pat dry. Air dry for about an hour. Smoke according to directions for your smoker, generally 6 to 8 hours.

Chicken Liver Pâté

(Sheila McQueen, Renowned English Flower Arranger)

½	pound chicken livers	1	teaspoon salt
1½	sticks butter (divided)	⅛	teaspoon cayenne pepper
3	tablespoons minced onion	¼	teaspoon mixed herbs (basil, tarragon, thyme)
1	garlic clove, minced		
⅛	cup water	1	tablespoon brandy

In a sauté pan, melt ½ of the butter. Add onions and garlic to butter and over low heat cook, stirring, until limp. Add livers and water and sauté until livers are just done. Put liver mixture in a food processor fitted with the steel blade along with the salt, cayenne, herbs, brandy and rest of the butter. Blend until smooth.

Pack pâté in a small crock and cover with a layer of clarified butter.

Pâté keeps well in the refrigerator and also freezes well.

Serves 15 to 20.

An interesting flavor can be inserted by cooking and blending 2 ounces chopped fresh mushrooms with the chicken livers.

Deep Fried Peanuts or Almonds

In small batches, cover shelled almonds or peanuts with boiling water. Let stand about 5 minutes until brown skins will slip off. With thumb and finger, remove brown skins. "Blanched" almonds describe nuts with the brown skins removed and are available in food stores; their use saves a good deal of effort. Let nuts dry thoroughly on paper towels - preferably overnight.

In a saucepan or deep fryer, heat vegetable oil until a cube of bread browns in 30 seconds (about 350 degrees). Put nuts in a frying basket about 2 layers deep and plunge in the hot oil. Cook until nuts are light brown. Almonds should cook in about 2 minutes; peanuts in 1 to 1½ minutes. Peanuts fried with the brown skins on have a different, but very good flavor.

Spread nuts on a double layer of paper towels. Sprinkle generously with salt and let cool. Pickling salt should be used if available. It is more finely ground and the secret of really tasty nuts. Store nuts in air tight containers for as long as 2 weeks.

Salted nuts are extremely popular with cocktails or as general snack food. When it comes to adding nuts to other dishes, however, a bright caution flag should be displayed. Even with deference to texture, nuts go too far and add a discordant note in most instances.

Slivered almonds and pine nuts (which are not really nuts) may be exceptions, but otherwise I prefer my food without nuts, particularly walnuts.

Roasted Pecans or Almonds

2   **pounds shelled pecans or 2 pounds blanched almonds (i.e., with the brown skins removed)**

¾   **stick butter (or margarine)**
Salt to taste

Spread nuts in a cookie pan, not more than 2 layers thick. Dot with butter cut in ¼ inch slices (about 1 tablespoon of butter per 2 cups of nuts). Bake nuts in a preheated 250 degree oven. When butter is melted stir nuts and salt liberally. Thereafter, stir every 30 minutes or so. Add more salt, if needed. After nuts have baked for 2 hours, cool a couple of nuts and test for crispness. Continue testing every half hour until nuts reach the desired crispness (generally about 2½ hours). Almonds cook a little faster than pecans. Be especially careful not to scorch almonds.

Nuts will keep for a couple of weeks in airtight tins.

Game Bird Terrine

Dove and quail (uncooked) sufficient to make 20 ounces of meat (12 dove breasts and 12 whole quail will produce the amount of meat required, but the proportion of dove and quail may be varied depending on availability).

1 cup brandy (divided)

6-8 shallots, peeled and finely chopped (about ¾ cup) (divided)

1¼ pounds ground veal, approximate

½ pound pork fat (fat part of bacon may be used)

½ cup chopped and lightly packed parsley

1 tablespoon salt

1 teaspoon black pepper

2 teaspoons crumbled dried thyme leaves

⅛ teaspoon ground cloves

¼ teaspoon ground nutmeg

½ teaspoon ground ginger

12 juniper berries, crushed

3 eggs

4 bay leaves

Strips of blanched bacon (about 1 pound)

Skin and bone the birds, keeping breasts intact. Slice breasts in ¼ inch strips longwise and marinate overnight, or longer, in ¼ cup brandy and ¼ cup chopped shallots. Refrigerate rest of bird meat including all little scraps (should have 12 ounces sliced breast meat and 8 ounces scraps or moderately more of each).

In a food processor fitted with the steel blade, process the meat scraps and the ground veal (a total of 1¾ pounds-adjust amount of veal accordingly) until smooth. Add pork fat and process again.

Add parsley, seasonings, eggs and remaining shallots and brandy, plus the brandy and shallots from the marinade. Process thoroughly. In a hot skillet, sauté small patties (about 1 tablespoon) of the mixture (known as "forcemeat") and check for salt, brandy and other seasoning (seasoning tastes less when cold). Add more seasoning to taste.

Line a 2 quart oblong casserole dish (with lid) with blanched bacon slices, leaving slices hanging over sides to cover top. Cover bacon with approximately ½ of the forcemeat. Then arrange the bird breast slices, in a lengthwise direction, on top of the forcemeat. Top the breast slices with the rest of the forcemeat. Lay 4 bay leaves on top layer of forcemeat and fold the bacon slices over the top. Cover casserole with aluminum foil and put on the lid.

Game Bird Terrine continued

Place the casserole in a roasting pan with enough water to come half way up the side of the casserole and bake in a preheated 350 degree oven for 1½ hours. Remove the roasting pan from the oven, but leave the casserole in the water. Remove cover and leave foil in place. Place a couple of bricks (or other heavy objects) evenly on foil and leave for a few hours. Then remove the casserole from the water and put in the refrigerator overnight, bricks and all. Bricks may be removed the next day.

It is best to refrigerate the terrine for a couple of days to meld flavors. The terrine will keep in the refrigerator for a couple of weeks and freezes well.

Pheasant or wild duck may be substituted for the birds in this recipe.

Roadside fruit stand, Kenya, Africa.

Sardine Rolls

2   cans (about 4 ounces each) skinless and boneless sardines

2½ tablespoons Worcestershire sauce

2   tablespoons lemon juice

3   tablespoons mayonnaise

¼ teaspoon salt

3   dashes hot sauce

Discard liquid from the sardine cans and mash sardines. Add the remaining ingredients and continue mashing to form a smooth paste. Remove crust from a loaf of white bread and slice very thin. (Special devices are available in cookware stores to slice regular slices of bread in half.)

Spread about 1 level tablespoon of the sardine spread across middle of each slice of bread. Roll the slice up and secure with a flat tooth pick. Bake rolls in a preheated 300 degree oven until nicely browned (10 to 12 minutes).

May cook rolls until lightly browned and freeze. Then reheat rolls until nicely browned.

Makes 25 to 30 rolls.

The sardine spread that goes in these rolls is also delicious served with crackers as a dip.

Blanched Vegetables

Fresh vegetables are blanched by plunging small batches in boiling water for a short period of time. Vegetables are generally pared and cut into bite size pieces before blanching. Cauliflower, broccoli, asparagus, green beans, snow peas, carrots and squash are excellent.

Recommended blanching times:

Cauliflower - 2 minutes

Broccoli - 2 minutes

Asparagus - 3-5 minutes

Green beans - 3-4 minutes

Snow peas - ½ minute

Carrots - 3 minutes

Squash - 2 minutes

Refresh vegetables in cold water after blanching and hold in refrigerator until ready to use.

Artichoke Pickles

(Consi Mallory's)

7 quarts Jerusalem artichokes	Very small hot red peppers
3 quarts onions (about 4 pounds) (white onions about the size of lemons work particularly well)	

Wash artichokes (a clothes washing machine at low speed will do most of the job). Trim off roots, sprouts and bad spots. Peel onions.

Cut artichokes and onions in bite-size pieces. Measure artichokes and onions after they have been cut up. Sterilize pint or quart mason jars and lids. Pack each jar tightly with pro-rata part of artichokes and onions and one small red pepper, if desired.

Sauce

6 pounds sugar	1½ ounces dry mustard (1 box)
5 quarts cider vinegar	2½ tablespoons turmeric (⅓ box)
1⅓ cups salt	

Bring sauce to a rolling boil. Fill packed jars nearly to top with boiling sauce (about 4 jars at a time). Wipe rims and seal at once.

Store at least 6 weeks to let flavors meld. Pickles will keep for a year or more.

Makes 20 pints.

Jerusalem artichokes have nothing to do with Jerusalem, nor are they related to the better known globe artichoke. They are a relative of the sunflower and the artichokes themselves are tubers on the roots.

Consi Mallory, one of Atlanta's premier home cooks, was the source of this recipe. She loved food and loved to cook. Moreover, she was extremely generous in passing on her secrets to aspiring friends. These pickles are outstanding as an hors d'oeuvre during the cocktail hour.

Artichoke Relish

(Magnolia Club, West Point, Georgia)

This recipe came from the Magnolia Club in West Point, Georgia. There West Point Manufacturing Company (later West Point-Pepperell) housed its customers and other visitors. The Club set a beautiful table and this relish, made by a local cook, added zest to many meals.

4	quarts Jerusalem artichokes	1	quart onions
2	pounds cabbage	½	cup salt
6	large green bell peppers or 10 large banana peppers (about 1½ quarts)		

Sauce

2	quarts cider vinegar	1	tablespoon black pepper
2½	pounds sugar	1	tablespoon turmeric
4	tablespoons mustard seed	1	jar French's prepared mustard (9 ounce)
¾	cup flour		

Clean artichokes well. Putting them in clothes washer at low speed will do most of job. Trim off roots, sprouts and bad spots. Slice artichokes very thin (2 mm blade in a food processor). Cover sliced artichokes with water and refrigerate 12 to 48 hours.

Remove core and heavy outer leaves from cabbage. Remove core and stems from green peppers. Peel onions. Slice cabbage, peppers and onions very thin (2 mm blade in a food processor). Sprinkle vegetables with the salt, cover with cold water and refrigerate 3 to 5 hours. Measure vegetables after they have been sliced.

In a large pot, mix vinegar, sugar and mustard seed. Bring to boil. Drain the soaking vegetables (do not rinse). Add vegetables to the boiling vinegar solution.

In a small bowl mix the flour, pepper, turmeric and prepared mustard. Add a little of the boiling liquid to the mustard mixture stirring until it is thin enough to pour.

Promptly after the vegetables have been added to the boiling vinegar solution, stir in the mustard mixture. Continue stirring until well blended. (Do not stir mustard mixture into boiling sauce before adding the vegetables; the heat will cause lumps to form.) Return pickles to a boil, stirring constantly. Cut off heat immediately. Pour pickles into sterilized jars, wipe rims and seal.

Makes about 14 pints.

*At a Rome food bazaar, a kindly salesman demonstrates
long, lemon peel spirals for our granddaughter, Emily.*

Soups

Sidewalk in a small town on the Russian inland waterway.

Soups

Soup is a fine addition to any menu. With the increased popularity of cold soup, it knows no season. Even so, most meals today have a limited number of courses, and the inclusion of soup must be balanced against the presence of an appetizer, salad or even a dessert.

Some of the most delicious soups are almost a meal in themselves. Wild Duck Gumbo, p.54, Black Bean Soup, p.40, and Galacian Soup, p.48, come to mind. Such soups should be the focus of the meal joined by one or two light courses – a salad and dessert for example.

A more substantial meal may still be enhanced by soup. Then it is best to turn to a light number; among my favorites are Bloody Bull Soup, p.39, Cold Cucumber Soup, p.44, and Yellow Tomato Gazpacho, p.50.

Making fresh pasta, Municipal Market, Oxford, England.

Bloody Bull Soup

1   can chicken bouillon (12 ounce)
    (or 3 chicken bouillon cubes dissolved
    in 12 ounces water)
1   can tomato juice (12 ounce)
1   can beef consommé (12 ounce)
½   cup orange juice

1   red apple, sliced
1   medium onion, sliced
½   teaspoon salt
¼   teaspoon black pepper
½   cup dry sherry
1   cup whipping cream

Tomato, orange, apple and onion may be strange bedfellows, but this unusual combination makes a truly remarkable soup. Highly recommended.

Put all ingredients except sherry and cream in a saucepan and boil hard for 10 minutes. Strain and add sherry. Whip cream and stir into soup. Heat soup and serve.

Serves 6.

Avocado Soup

3   cups chicken stock
1   large ripe avocado, coarsely chopped
    (about 1 cup)
½   medium onion, coarsely chopped
    (about ¾ cup)
1   tablespoon Worcestershire sauce

2   dashes hot sauce
2   tablespoons olive oil
½   teaspoon salt
⅛   teaspoon white pepper
1   tablespoon lime juice
    Parsley or chives for garnish

Put all ingredients, except parsley or chives, in a blender fitted with the steel blade and blend well until smooth. Serve soup ice cold, garnished with chopped chives or parsley.

Serves 5.

For a richer soup you may stir in 1 cup heavy cream and correct the seasoning.

Black Bean Soup

1	pound black beans	2	cloves garlic, chopped
3	green bell peppers, seeded and sliced	⅔	pound salt pork, cut in 1 to 2 inch chunks
2	medium onions, sliced	24	black peppercorns

Wash beans well. Soak in water to cover several hours or overnight. Put beans in a soup pot with 4 quarts water. Add bell peppers, onions, garlic, salt pork and peppercorns. Bring to a boil and simmer 3 hours, about half the time without a top, until soup thickens.

Then in an iron skillet put:

¾	cup olive oil	2	cloves garlic, finely chopped
⅔	pound salt pork, cut in ¼ inch dice	4	bay leaves

Fry out the salt pork until well done. Then, add contents of the skillet to soup pot and simmer soup another hour or so.

Discard chunks of pork. Then, press soup through a coarse sieve, or put through a food mill, discarding bean skins and other solids. At this point the soup freezes well.

When ready to use, reheat the soup and add:

4 ounces sherry or Madeira

The soup should be served in soup bowls over white rice topped with freshly chopped onion, about 2 tablespoons onion per bowl.

Since making this soup takes some time, it is a good idea to cook a double batch and freeze part for future use.

Serves 10.

About Salt and Black Pepper

Salt and particularly black pepper are available in a wide range of grinds, ordinary, iodized table salt serves most purposes. Coarsely ground sea salt, however, accentuates the flavor of some dishes, such as grilled meat and roasted peppers. I have not experimented with exotic salts with particular flavors that are beginning to appear in the market.

Black pepper comes in a fine grind, regular grind and several coarse grinds. A pepper mill will provide a range of grinds for many recipes that are improved by freshly ground pepper. For example, grilled meat and some salads demand coarsely ground pepper. Fine or regular grind is much preferred for seasoning flour and meal as the coarser varieties do not adhere well. Elsewhere the selection is a matter of taste.

At table, The French tend to serve extremely finely ground salt and black pepper. These grinds may blend better in some delicate sauces, but they come up short in providing real zest to a meal.

Lady selling flowers in a small Russian village.

Borsch

(Beet Soup)

½ cup carrots, cut in fine julienne strips
1 cup thinly slivered onion
1 cup beet juice
2 cups beef stock (or beef broth)
1 tablespoon butter
1 cup finely shredded cabbage
3 tablespoons cider vinegar

3 cups cooked whole beets, fine julienne strips (24 ounces canned beats; julienne strips are now available under the name "shoestring beets")
½ teaspoon salt
⅛ teaspoon black pepper
6 tablespoons sour cream
6 tablespoons finely chopped cucumber

Cut all julienne strips in 1½ inch lengths.

In a saucepan barely cover carrots and onions with water, bring to a boil and simmer covered about 20 minutes (until carrots are tender). Add beet juice, beef stock, butter, cabbage, salt, pepper and vinegar. Continue simmering for about 10 minutes; add beets and cook 5 minutes more.

Serve soup hot or cold in individual bowls. To each bowl of soup add 1 tablespoon sour cream and 1 tablespoon chopped cucumbers.

If you make your own beef stock, cut all meat scraps off the bones and add to the soup.

Serves 8.

Bahamian Conch Chowder

(Cumberland House, Nassau)

1½ pounds conch meat (6 to 8 conchs)

1½ sticks butter

2 medium green bell peppers, cored, seeded and cut in chunks

2 medium onions, coarsely chopped

1 large carrot, scraped and cut in thick slices

¼ cup lime juice (2 to 3 limes)

5 ounces tomato paste

1 can whole peeled tomatoes and juice (16 ounce)

2 cups crumbled saltines (or 1 pound peeled and diced potatoes)

½ teaspoon salt (more if you substitute potatoes)

1 teaspoon black pepper

1½-2 teaspoons thyme leaves

3 bay leaves

1 pint beef stock or beef bouillon

1 pint water

1½ cups dry sherry

Cut conch in chunks and put through a meat grinder or chop in a food processor fitted with the steel blade, (conch should be about the texture of hamburger). Melt butter in a large skillet, add conch and simmer, stirring occasionally, until the conch takes on a little color (about 10 minutes).

In food processor fitted with the steel blade, chop bell peppers, onions and carrots until about the texture of cole slaw. Stir lime juice into conch meat; then add chopped bell peppers, onions and carrots. Simmer until vegetables are limp. Transfer to a soup pot. Add all other ingredients except sherry and simmer for 1¼ hours. Stir occasionally and add water as needed. Do not cook longer because conch will get tough.

Before serving, stir in sherry and correct seasoning. If not using all of the soup, stir in about 1 tablespoon of sherry per cup of soup.

The soup freezes well, but wait and add sherry after reheating.

Makes 2½ to 3 quarts.

Serves 12.

Florida Keys Conch Chowder

This recipe for Conch Chowder is tomato-beef based reminiscent of the great chowder served by Marker Eight Restaurant in the Florida Keys.

6	conchs (about 3 cups chopped)	1	teaspoon thyme leaves
2	green bell peppers (medium)	1	can whole tomatoes, peeled (28 ounce)
1	carrot (large)	3	ounces tomato paste
2	onions (large)	2	cups saltines, crumbled
½	stick butter	1½	quarts beef stock (or half water, half beef bouillon)
¾	teaspoon salt		
½	teaspoon black pepper	2	cups dry sherry

In a food processor fitted with the steel blade (or meat grinder), chop conch, peppers, carrot and onions (until about the texture of hamburger). In a large sauté pan, cook the mixture in the butter, stirring frequently, until well mixed, heated through and the conch takes on a little color (7 to 10 minutes). Season with salt, pepper and thyme. Add tomatoes, tomato paste and saltines. Add beef stock (should be enough to cover ingredients) and simmer the soup for 1 hour.

Just before serving, add sherry.

Freezes well.

Serves 16.

Cold Cucumber Soup

4	medium cucumbers, peeled, seeded and cut in chucks	½	teaspoon salt
		¼	teaspoon white pepper
2	medium onions, coarsely chopped	1	pint whipping cream
4	cups chicken stock		Chives for garnish

You should have a generous 4 cups each of cucumbers and onions. Put cucumbers and onions in a saucepan with the chicken stock, salt and pepper; bring to a boil; cover and simmer for about 15 minutes. Do not overcook as cucumbers will loose their flavor.

In a food processor fitted with the steel blade, blend soup in batches until smooth. Chill. Stir chilled cream into soup. Correct seasoning. Serve soup in bowls with finely chopped fresh cucumber and chopped chives as garnish. Before adding cream, you may freeze soup for later use.

Serves 8 to 10.

Cucumber and Spinach Soup

2 tablespoons butter

1 large bunch green onions (about 12), coarsely chopped including ½ of green tops

2 medium cucumbers, peeled, seeded and coarsely chopped

3 cups strong chicken stock

1 package frozen leaf spinach (10 ounce)

1 tablespoon lemon juice

⅜ teaspoon salt

¼ teaspoon white pepper (scant)

½ cup whipping cream

¼ cup milk

Slices of cucumber and radish for garnish

In a saucepan melt butter and cook scallions slowly until just tender. Add cucumbers and sauté slowly for about 5 minutes (stir frequently). Add stock and simmer until cucumbers are tender (15 to 20 minutes). Add spinach which has been thawed and large stems removed. Return to a simmer and cook 5 minutes more. Add lemon juice, salt and pepper and puree in batches in a food processor fitted with the steel blade. Stir in cream and milk. Serve hot or cold with a slice of cucumber and radish in each bowl.

Soup freezes well before adding cream and milk. If soup has been frozen, thaw, stir in cream and milk and heat or chill thoroughly.

Serves 6.

Peruvian woman braiding onions.

Cold Curried Soup

3½	cups chicken stock	2	cups whipping cream
1	teaspoon medium curry powder (more or less)	4	chunks chutney
⅓	teaspoon salt	2	tablespoons chopped roasted peanuts
¼	teaspoon white pepper	12	thin slices cucumber
3	egg yolks	1	hard-boiled egg, grated
		2	tablespoons finely chopped onion

Bring the chicken stock to a boil and stir in curry powder, salt and white pepper. With a fork beat egg yolks; stir ½ cup hot stock into egg yolks; and then blend with cream.

Add the cream mixture to the chicken stock and stir constantly over low heat until the soup is almost to a simmer (8 to 10 minutes). Remove soup from heat and continue stirring for a minute or two. Do not let the soup come to a boil as eggs will curdle. Chill soup in the refrigerator.

Taste for seasoning.

Serve soup in individual soup bowls. To each bowl add:

Generous chunk of chutney
Chopped peanuts
Chopped onion
2-3 slices cucumber with grated hard-boiled egg sprinkled on top.

The accompaniments make this dish!

Serves 5 to 6.

Roasted Eggplant Soup

2	medium eggplants	1½-2	cups half-and-half
8	cloves garlic	½	cup sherry
	Olive oil	1	teaspoon thyme leaves
1	cup chopped onion	½	teaspoon salt
3-4	cups chicken stock	¼	teaspoon black pepper

Cut eggplants in half lengthwise. Insert split garlic cloves in cut sides of the eggplants (make incisions with a sharp knife as needed). Drizzle cut sides with olive oil and sprinkle with salt and pepper. Bake in a preheated 275 degree oven for 3 hours or so.

Sauté onions in a little olive oil until limp. Scrape out eggplant pulp including garlic (should be about 2 cups). In a food processor fitted with the steel blade, puree pulp and onions. (Optional: strain out eggplant seeds if they seem large.) Add thyme, salt and pepper.

Heat stock in a saucepan and stir in the eggplant puree. Can freeze soup at this point or you can freeze puree before adding the stock. When ready to serve (either hot or cold), add half-and-half and sherry. Adjust seasoning.

Serves 8.

For a lighter soup, you may add an additional 1½ cups chicken stock instead of the half-and-half.

Galacian Soup

(Caldo Gallego from the Province of Galacia, Spain)

1½ cups dry white navy beans

⅓ pound salt pork, cut in ¼ inch dice

⅓ pound cooked smoked ham, cut in ¼ inch dice

⅓ pound chorizo (Spanish sausage), cut in ⅛ inch slices

1 ham bone

1½ teaspoons ground cumin

4 bay leaves

¼ teaspoon black pepper

½ pound tender turnip greens (heavy stems removed before weighing)

2½ cups new potatoes, peeled and cut in ¼ inch dice

Soak navy beans in about 6 cups cold water overnight.

Put diced salt pork in a large stock pot over low heat and brown pork lightly on all sides. Add ham and chorizo and brown on all sides. Drain the beans and add to the pot with 2 quarts water, the ham bone, cumin, bay leaves and pepper. Bring to a boil and simmer soup covered 1½ to 2 hours until the beans are tender.

Chop greens coarsely. Add greens and potatoes to soup and simmer 20 to 30 minutes longer. If frozen spinach is used, wait and add about 10 minutes before the soup is ready.

To give soup a little more substance mash a few of the potatoes and return to the pot. You may add more water if needed.

Remove the ham bone, correct seasoning and serve. The flavor of the soup improves if kept in the refrigerator for a day or so. Freezes well.

A warming soup for the cold winter months, Caldo Gallego still has a spring freshness.

Serves 8 to 10.

Fresh kale greens or a 10 ounce package of frozen spinach may be substituted for the turnip greens.

Gazpacho

1 medium garlic clove, chopped

1 heaping teaspoon salt

1 medium yellow onion, chopped (about 2 cups)

3 tablespoons white wine vinegar

4 tablespoons olive oil

¼ teaspoon white pepper

4 ripe tomatoes, peeled and seeded

2 cups tomato juice and/or beef bouillon

For an interesting touch, combine tomato juice and 2 teaspoons prepared horseradish in an ice cube tray. Freeze and use cubes in the soup instead of ice.

Mash garlic and salt and put in food processor fitted with the steel blade along with the onion, vinegar, olive oil and pepper. Blend until smooth. Add tomatoes and tomato juice and/or bouillon. Blend until well combined. Correct seasoning.

Serve ice cold in bowls with an ice cube in each.

Pass two or three side dishes of finely chopped:

Tomato

Cucumber

Green pepper

Spring onions

For variety yellow tomatoes with bouillon work well in this gazpacho recipe.

Serves 5 to 6.

A red toadstool, probably poisonous, near the Ponoi River, Russia.

Yellow Tomato Gazpacho

This recipe for Yellow Tomato Gazpacho is well known at Atlanta's Capital City Club. The chef decorates each bowl of soup with a delicate petal design using tomato ketchup in a pastry tube.

1	pound yellow bell peppers		⅓	cup mayonnaise
1½	pounds yellow tomatoes, peeled and seeded		2	tablespoons olive oil
1	pound cucumbers, peeled and seeded		2	tablespoons white wine vinegar
½	cup chopped sweet onion (preferably Vidalia)		1	teaspoon salt
2	medium cloves garlic, coarsely chopped		⅓	teaspoon white pepper
1½	slices white bread (crusts removed)		3	dashes hot sauce
			1	red tomato, finely chopped for garnish

Roast peppers over open flame until blackened; remove skin, interior ribs and seeds. Put all the ingredients, except red tomato for garnish, in a food processor fitted with the steel blade and process until smooth.

Store soup in the refrigerator for several hours. If too thick, thin with a few ice cubes.

Garnish with the red tomato.

Olive bread is a nice accompaniment.

Serves 6.

Cream of Mushroom Soup

3	tablespoons butter		⅓	teaspoon ground nutmeg
1	pound mushrooms, finely chopped		½	teaspoon salt
½	medium onion, finely chopped		⅓	teaspoon black pepper
2	cups milk		2	tablespoons lemon juice
2	cups half-and-half		3	tablespoons sherry

In a sauté pan over medium heat, cook mushrooms and onions in butter for 7 to 8 minutes, stirring frequently. Mix in the milk and half-and-half; add nutmeg, salt, pepper, lemon juice and sherry; heat to just boiling and serve.

Serves 6.

You may substitute beef bouillon for the milk and cream to make a lighter soup. You may also vary the proportion of milk and half-and-half.

Gazpacho Andaluz

¾ cup cucumber, peeled and diced (coarse seeds removed)

¼ green pepper, seeded and diced

½ cup chopped onion

1 large clove garlic, chopped

1 teaspoon salt

¼ cup olive oil

Juice of 1 lemon

3 tablespoons white wine vinegar

2 slices day-old French bread (soaked in water)

4 medium tomatoes, seeded and quartered (can peel tomatoes, but hurts color and flavor to some extent)

In blender fitted with the steel blade, blend foregoing ingredients, except bread and tomatoes, until smooth. Add bread and tomatoes and blend. Chill thoroughly.

Serve in soup bowls with an ice cube in each and pass a selection of the following accompaniments:

Tomato, finely chopped

Cucumber, finely chopped

Spring onions, finely chopped

Green pepper, finely chopped

Small croutons, fried in olive oil

Pimento stuffed green olives, sliced

An old recipe suggests topping this gazpacho with chopped hard-boiled egg and chopped bacon.

Serves 4.

She Crab Soup

½	stick butter	¼	cup crab roe
2	tablespoons finely chopped onion	⅛	teaspoon mace
¼	cup cracker crumbs	½	teaspoon salt
2	cups milk	¼	teaspoon black pepper
2	cups cream	6	tablespoons sherry
2	cups white crabmeat (preferably lump)		

Melt butter in a saucepan. Add onion and cook until limp but not browned. Add crumbs and heat. Blend in milk, cream and then crabmeat and crab roe, if used. Add mace, salt and pepper. Bring just to a boil and stir in sherry. Serve at once.

This soup derives its name from the crab roe. You are not likely to find it, however, unless you pick your own crabs. The roe will not be missed if unavailable.

Serves 6.

Tomato-Dill Soup

3	large ripe tomatoes, peeled and seeded (about 2 cups) (or 15 ounce can peeled tomatoes)	⅛	teaspoon black pepper
		2	sprays fresh dill (about 1 tablespoon packed)
1	large onion, sliced (about 1 cup)	1	tablespoon tomato paste
1	clove garlic, sliced	¼	cup cold water
¾	teaspoon salt	1	cup chicken stock

Simmer the above ingredients, except the chicken stock, covered for 15 minutes. Then process the soup in a food processor fitted with the steel blade until smooth. Add chicken stock, reheat, correct seasoning and serve.

Serves 3 to 4.

Vichyssoise

¼	cup butter	2	cups cream
1	cup thinly sliced leeks (white parts only)	1	teaspoon salt
⅓	cup thinly sliced onion	¼	teaspoon white pepper
1	quart chicken stock	3	tablespoons chives, finely chopped for garnish
3	cups thinly sliced potatoes		

Melt butter, add leaks and onion and cook, stirring constantly, until onions are soft. Add stock, potatoes and salt; cook until potatoes are tender; rub through a fine sieve or put through a food mill. (If you prefer, soup can be processed in a blender fitted with the steel blade.) Return soup to heat, add pepper and mix well. Chill thoroughly. Stir in cream and garnish with chives.

Serves 8 to 10.

If leeks are not available, substitute an additional ⅔ cup onion.

Burro drawn cart, Luxor, Egypt.

Wild Duck Gumbo

8   small or 5 large wild ducks
      (or 3 dozen dove breasts)
1   onion, sliced
1½ cups sliced celery with tops

4   bay leaves
1   teaspoon salt
1   teaspoon black peppercorns
3   tablespoons cider vinegar

Pick and clean ducks. Put ducks in a pot and cover with water; add above ingredients and parboil about 1 hour. Skim off froth as it rises. Remove ducks; strain and reserve 3 quarts of the stock.

1   cup flour
1   cup oil
2   cups coarsely chopped onion
2   cups seeded and coarsely chopped
      green peppers
2   cups coarsely chopped celery
2   pounds Andouille, Kielbasa or other
      smoked sausage, cut in ¼ inch rounds

4   tablespoons Worcestershire sauce
6   dashes hot sauce
1   teaspoon black pepper
6   cloves garlic, peeled
⅛ teaspoon sage
½ teaspoon thyme leaves
1   teaspoon garlic salt
    Gumbo filé

Make dark brown roux with flour and oil, Microwave Roux, p.55. If not made in an iron skillet, transfer roux to one and add onion, green peppers and celery and sauté slowly until vegetables are limp.

Transfer roux and vegetables to a stock pot and add 3 quarts strained duck stock and the garlic cloves. Boil slowly for 30 minutes or so, uncovered. Remove duck meat from skin and bones and cut into bite size pieces. Cook sausage in a hot skillet to render fat. Drain.

To the stock pot add duck meat, sausage and seasonings, except gumbo filé. (Can add two 12 ounce cans tomatoes, if desired.) Simmer uncovered for about 1½ hours. Skim off oil as it bubbles up to the top.

Can refrigerate or freeze gumbo at this point.

Wild Duck Gumbo continued

Reheat gumbo and add:

20 ounces frozen sliced okra
12 spring onions, sliced (including part of tops)
¾   cup chopped parsley

If the gumbo has gotten too thick, add a little more duck stock. The gumbo should, however, have real substance. Simmer about 20 minutes, correct seasoning.

Serve in bowls over cooked white or wild rice. On each bowl, sprinkle about ¼ teaspoon gumbo filé.

You may freeze gumbo after it is fully cooked.

Gumbo is a fine way to remove aging ducks from your freezer.

Makes 6 quarts.

John Izard, Jr., Kate and south Georgia wood ducks.

Microwave Roux

1 cup flour   **1 cup vegetable oil**

In a 1 quart or larger microwave container, whisk the flour into the oil, combining well. The roux will boil over in a smaller container. A 1 or 2 quart Pyrex measuring cup works well because the handle stays cool.

Put container in microwave on high setting. Cook 8 to 9 minutes. Whisk well every 2 minutes. Depending on the recipe, the desired color of the roux may vary from the color of peanut butter to that of a walnut. When the roux has reached the desired shade of brown, transfer to an iron skillet for use or store in the refrigerator or freezer. The roux will keep for a couple of weeks or longer. If you reheat the roux, be careful not to let it scorch.

This basic roux is the foundation of much cajun cooking. It produces a distinctive flavor. The microwave eliminates the constant stirring required by the conventional slow cooking method and is every bit as good.

Salads

Vegetable cart, Rouen, France.

Salads

If forced to pick one category of food as my favorite, it would probably be salad, followed by meat and fish. Salad tends to be an all encompassing term, but I have definite ideas about real salads.

With just enough exceptions to prove the rule, I eliminate any sweet concoction starting with congealed Bing Cherry salad, anything with marshmallows, jello mixtures and a good many fruit salads. Nor am I partial to heavy combinations - three bean, macaroni, or rice salads. The absence of page references following these salads means that none are included in this cookbook! Exceptions such as Chicken Salad, p.63, and Niçoise Salad, p.67, are really main courses in themselves.

Where do these broad exclusions leave us? A salad should be light textured, tart and above all fresh. Crisp lettuce, cabbage, ripe tomatoes and avocados, watercress and a member of the onion family, are the infrastructure of many delicious salads. Not only should the vegetables be absolutely fresh, but each vegetable must be properly prepared. Wash individual lettuce leaves and twirl them dry. Tomatoes and avocados should be peeled and neatly sliced. Remove heavy stems from watercress and separate onion slices into individual rings.

The same rules apply to salad dressings. Sweet is out! Light dressings are preferred over creamy ones. Basic Oil and Vinegar Dressing, p.75, with its innumerable variations, is the standby. Tart, preferably homemade, Mayonnaise, p.72, also has its place.

In the early '50s, there were only three or four quality restaurants in the city of Atlanta. One of them, Escoe's, was the signature restaurant of a former chef at Atlanta's Capital City Club. His most popular salad, p.64, could not have been more simple, but its appeal came from the care of its preparation. Fresh, firm heads of iceberg lettuce were cored, stripped of their outer leaves and, with a sharp knife, cut into slices. About half as much red cabbage was prepared in the same manner. The lettuce and cabbage were immersed in ice water. Finally, carrots were peeled and cut in long slivers which were added to the ice water. After the vegetables had soaked in the ice water for an hour or so, they were drained and folded in a terry towel which was then kept in the refrigerator until time to serve the salad. To this day, I try to emulate this marvelous creation!

Avocados Nicaragua

3   large ripe avocados

12   lettuce leaves (approximate)

      Onion, finely chopped (in a small bowl)

2   lemons, cut in half

      White wine vinegar

Worcestershire sauce

Hot sauce

Olive oil

Salt shaker

Pepper grinder filled with whole black peppercorns

In the 1960's the clubs in Managua used this presentation for magnificent Nicaraguan avocados.

Cut avocados in half lengthwise and remove seeds. Put a couple of lettuce leaves on six salad plates and put an avocado half on each.

On a tray put the bowl of onion and the lemon halves; the bottles of vinegar, Worcestershire sauce, pepper sauce and olive oil; and the salt shaker and pepper grinder. Pass the tray and let each guest spoon some onion into the cavity of the avocado and then select the ingredients to be added. Any or all go very well with avocados. After part of the avocados have been eaten, pass the tray again.

Serves 6.

Avocado and Bacon Sandwich

2   slices white bread

      Mayonnaise

¼   avocado, sliced thin lengthwise

3   slices crisp bacon

3-4   lettuce leaves

      Salt

      Black pepper

A sandwich, perhaps with a soup or a salad, makes a fine informal lunch. Most delicatessens provide turkey, corned beef, pastrami and tuna along with various cheeses and an assortment of breads. I really have no suggestions to add to these customary combinations.

There are, however, a few special sandwiches that followed me home. They are collected in the Index under Sandwiches.

Toast regular sliced white bread and spread with mayonnaise. Arrange avocado and bacon slices on one piece of toast and top with lettuce leaves. Sprinkle with salt and pepper to taste and cover with the other slice of toast.

Jellied Cabbage Salad

4   tablespoons gelatin
     (4 envelopes, ¼ ounce each)

3   cups cold water (divided)

½   cup white wine vinegar

4   tablespoons lemon juice

1   teaspoon salt

3   dashes red pepper

2   cups cabbage, finely shredded and cut in
     ¾ inch lengths

⅓   cup finely diced onion

½   cup finely diced celery

½   cup finely diced green bell pepper

6   ounces sliced pimentos, slightly
     chopped and drained

In a small bowl stir gelatin into 1 cup of cold water until soft. Set bowl in a larger bowl of warm water until gelatin is well dissolved.

In a large bowl, mix vinegar, lemon juice, the other 2 cups cold water, salt, red pepper and dissolved gelatin. Put mixture in refrigerator until it begins to set (45 minutes to 1 hour).

Then stir in the cabbage, onion, celery, green pepper and pimentos.

Lightly wipe the inside of a 2 quart mold with a little vegetable oil (or use 2 one quart molds). Pour the mixture into the mold(s) and smooth top surface. Place mold(s) in the refrigerator for several hours, or overnight, until salad is firm. When ready to eat, unmold on lettuce leaves and serve with mayonnaise (preferably homemade).

A ring mold with the mayonnaise in a small bowl in the center makes an attractive presentation.

Serves 16 to 18.

Can make one half this recipe to serve 6 to 8.

About Caesar Salad

In 1924, Chef Caesar Cardini, working in a Tijuana, Mexico restaurant, invented Caesar Salad.

Chef Cardini always made the salad table side in a large wooden bowl. With a fork, the anchovies, garlic, salt, dry mustard and pepper were mashed to a paste. The lemon juice and Worcestershire sauce were blended in and then the olive oil was added. Finally the coddled egg was cracked and dropped from high above the bowl. Dressing made in the salad bowl produced much fresher flavors than dressing made in advance.

The creamy, emulsified dressing commonly served by restaurants today greatly detracts from the zestful taste of traditional Caesar Salad.

Peruvian village market.

Caesar Salad

2 garlic cloves, sliced
1 teaspoon dry mustard
1 teaspoon salt
½ teaspoon freshly ground black pepper
4 anchovy fillets
6 tablespoons lemon juice
2 tablespoons Worcestershire sauce
6 tablespoons olive oil

1 egg
½ cup Parmesan cheese, grated (divided)
2 heads romaine lettuce
2 cups croutons

Put garlic, mustard, salt, pepper and anchovies in a large salad bowl (preferably wooden). With a fork mash garlic and anchovies mixing with the dry ingredients until they form a thick paste. Then mix in the lemon juice and Worcestershire sauce and finally the olive oil. Mix thoroughly with a fork. Add egg and mix well again (egg may be omitted without any great loss). Stir in one half of the Parmesan cheese.

The light yellowish, green inner leaves of romaine make the most delectable salad (save the outer leaves for another use). Wash and crisp the leaves and break the larger ones in halves or thirds. Put the romaine in the bowl with the dressing and toss the leaves until well coated. Sprinkle on the rest of the Parmesan cheese and toss again. Lastly add the croutons.

Excellent croutons especially for Caesar Salad are available in supermarkets. Homemade croutons are even better. Remove the crusts from regular sliced white bread. Cut bread in ¼ inch dice. Cover the bottom of a cookie pan with olive oil and bake the croutons in a 250 degree oven until crisp. Stir croutons occasionally and add a bit more olive oil, if needed.

Serves 6.

*From her home garden,
Cabezon de la Sal, Spain.*

Chicken or Turkey Salad

2 cups cooked chicken or turkey, cut in ½ inch cubes

1 cup chopped celery

¼ cup finely chopped onion

2 tablespoons cider vinegar

Mayonnaise to blend

Salt and black pepper to taste

Mix chicken or turkey, celery and onion; sprinkle with vinegar; and let stand for a little while. Add enough mayonnaise to bind and season the salad with salt and pepper. Serve at once.

Serves 4.

All white meat makes a fancier chicken or turkey salad.

Cabezon de la Sal is a small town in northwestern Spain. Its name translates "Big head of salt," a reference to salt mines in the area at the time of the Roman Legions (100 A.D.).

Cole Slaw

½ head firm fresh cabbage

Ice water

Cut cabbage in half vertically. Then vertically cut the half in 3 or 4 wedges. Discard the wilted outer leaves. With a sharp knife finely sliver the thin cabbage leaves avoiding the heavy ribs around the core. The slivering can be done with the fine blade of a food processor, but I can do a better job with a good knife.

Cover the slivered cabbage with ice water including a few ice cubes and set aside for ½ to 1 hour. Then drain cabbage and pat dry with a towel. The soaking process makes the cabbage much crisper.

Toss the cabbage with Basic Oil and Vinegar Dressing, p.75, or Cooked Dressing for Cole Slaw, p.71. Either dressing makes delicious cole slaw.

This cole slaw is not to be confused with characteristic southern cole slaw. The latter includes shredded carrots and bell peppers with a sweet mayonnaise based dressing that produces soggy slaw with a cloying flavor.

Greek Cucumber and Sour Cream

(Salad or Dip)

½ cup yogurt

½ cup sour cream

2 cloves garlic, minced

1 cucumber, peeled, seeded and finely chopped

Salt and white pepper to taste

Oregano to taste

Mix yogurt and sour cream. Then mix well with the cucumber and garlic. Add salt, white pepper and a little oregano.

Serves 4.

Escoe's Lettuce, Cabbage and Carrot Salad

1 medium head iceberg lettuce

1 small head red cabbage

2 large carrots

Remove outer leaves and core from lettuce. Cut head in ¾ inch slices keeping slices intact. Remove outer leaves and core from cabbage and cut in ⅜ inch slices. Scrape carrots and using a vegetable peeler, cut them in long slivers (slivers should be as thick as you can cut them with the peeler). Soak all of the cut-up vegetables in ice water for ½ to 1 hour and then dry salad in a terry towel. Keep salad wrapped in the towel in the refrigerator until ready to serve.

Dressing

4 medium cloves garlic, thinly sliced

1 teaspoon salt

¼ teaspoon freshly ground black pepper

⅓ cup red wine vinegar

⅔ cup olive oil

Put all ingredients in a jar with a lid, shake well and let blend for several hours or overnight.

Arrange salad on individual salad plates keeping the lettuce and cabbage slices pretty well in tact. Sprinkle with the dressing. Serve immediately.

Serves 6.

Lusco's Iceberg Lettuce Salad

1   **firm head iceberg lettuce**

This recipe was inspired by a salad served at Lusco's, a renowned restaurant in the heart of Mississippi's wild duck country – hence the name.

Discard tough outer leaves from the head of lettuce and cut out the core. Tear the head into bite-size pieces and put in a salad bowl.

Dressing

3   **tablespoons finely chopped green olives (pimento-stuffed olives are fine)**

2   **tablespoons finely chopped black olives**

3   **tablespoons finely chopped onion**

¾   **teaspoon minced garlic**

7-8 **anchovy fillets, cut in ¼ inch pieces**

3   **tablespoons lemon juice**

⅓   **cup olive oil**

¼   **teaspoon freshly ground black pepper**

    Salt to taste

Mix all ingredients except olive oil, pepper and salt. Then stir in olive oil and pepper plus salt, if needed.

Just before serving toss lettuce and dressing until thoroughly mixed.

Serves 8.

As a variation, you can add freshly ground Parmesan cheese to taste.

Bored vegetable salesman.

Pickled Green Beans

In the 1950's, the deli counter in the old Dinkler Plaza Hotel, Atlanta, featured a large jar of these outstanding pickled beans. They were offered to luncheon customers with their sandwiches or cold cuts.

16 ounces canned green string beans, drained
4 large cloves garlic, sliced
½ teaspoon crushed red peppers
1 teaspoon whole black peppercorns
1 ½ teaspoons mustard seed
1 teaspoon celery seed
1 ½ teaspoons salt
½ cup red wine vinegar
½ cup olive oil

Canned beans labeled "Great Lake Green Beans" work particularly well in this recipe.

In a large bowl, mix all ingredients together and allow to stand in the refrigerator for at least 36 hours.

Mushroom Salad

6-8 large fresh mushroom caps
½ cup diced celery
½ cup diced bell pepper (yellow, red or green)
¼ cup red onion, diced
1 small head leaf lettuce, broken in bite size pieces
4 tablespoons olive oil
2 tablespoons red wine vinegar
2 tablespoons lemon juice
½ teaspoon salt
¼ teaspoon black pepper
Lettuce leaves for garnish

Wash mushrooms and slice very thin vertically. Combine mushrooms, celery, bell pepper, onion and lettuce.

Mix olive oil, vinegar, lemon juice, salt and pepper. Toss dressing with mushroom mixture until well coated. Mound salad on a plate covered with lettuce leaves.

Serves 4.

Niçoise Salad

1 medium head Boston or Romaine lettuce, separated, washed, broken into pieces and thoroughly dried

2-3 medium-sized potatoes, boiled, drained, cut into ¼ inch slices and cooled

Salt and freshly ground black pepper to taste

1½ cups cooked string beans, cooled (about ½ pound)

18 ounces canned tuna fish, solid pack (preferably the imported variety, packed in olive oil), drained

6 anchovy fillets, drained

4 hard-boiled eggs, cooled and halved or quartered

2 large or 4 small ripe tomatoes, quartered

8 black olives, preferably the imported Niçoise variety

8 stuffed green olives

3 thin yellow onion slices

¼ cup red wine vinegar

½ cup olive oil

Place the lettuce leaves in a glass salad bowl. Spread the potato slices over the lettuce, sprinkle lightly with salt and pepper, and scatter the string beans on top. Make a mound of tuna fish in the center. Circle with the olives. Place the anchovies, eggs and tomatoes around the perimeter of the bowl, intersecting them with the olives as fancifully as you like. Separate onion slices into rings and scatter over the salad. (Capers may also be scattered on the salad if you like their flavor.) Cover the bowl with plastic wrap and refrigerate until ready to serve.

Dressing

¼ cup red wine vinegar

½ cup olive oil

½ teaspoon salt

⅛ teaspoon (heaping) freshly ground black pepper

In a small bowl, whisk together the vinegar, olive oil, salt and pepper. Pour the dressing over the salad and serve at once.

Serves 6 to 8.

Niçoise Salad (the author's presentation).

French Potato Salad

6	medium potatoes	White wine vinegar
2	medium onions, sliced horizontally very thin	Salt
	Olive oil	Freshly ground black pepper
		Parsley for garnish

In this recipe, Yukon Gold potatoes or new potatoes which remain firm after boiling work better than baking potatoes which tend to become mealy.

Boil potatoes in their skins until just tender. Peel, or not, as desired (I prefer them peeled). While still warm, slice potatoes thin. Line a glass bowl with a layer of sliced potatoes; then a layer of sliced onions. After each layer of potatoes, drizzle with olive oil and white wine vinegar and sprinkle with salt and pepper. Finish with a layer of potatoes.

Garnish with parsley and chill before serving.

Serves 6 to 8.

Sour Cream and Parsley Potato Salad

(Sallie Broyles)

2	cups sour cream	¼	teaspoon black pepper
2	cups mayonnaise	4	dashes hot sauce
3	tablespoons cream style horseradish	3	cups very thinly sliced onions
4	tablespoons white wine vinegar	9	cups thinly sliced boiled potatoes
1¼	teaspoons salt	½	cup chopped parsley (packed down)

Mix sour cream, mayonnaise, horseradish, vinegar, salt, pepper and hot sauce.

In a glass salad bowl, put a layer of potatoes, then one of onions and spread with a generous layer of the sour cream mixture. Sprinkle with parsley. Repeat layers until bowl is full (ending with parsley covering the top). Chill thoroughly.

Serves 10 to 12.

Wilted Spinach Salad

6   slices bacon
2   cloves garlic, thinly sliced
1   teaspoon dry mustard
1   tablespoon flour
1½ teaspoons sugar
½   cup red wine vinegar

⅛   teaspoon salt
⅛   teaspoon freshly ground black pepper
1   pound (2 quarts) crisp, young spinach, well washed
3   hard-boiled eggs, chopped

In a frying pan, cook bacon until crisp. Remove bacon and set aside. Put pan with bacon grease (about 4 tablespoons) over low heat and add sliced garlic. After a couple of minutes, whisk in dry mustard, flour and sugar. Then gradually whisk in vinegar. Season with salt and pepper and remove pan from the heat. If dressing is too thick, thin with a little warm water.

Add spinach to hot pan and toss until wilted and well coated with dressing. Add chopped eggs and crumble reserved bacon over the salad.

Serves 6.

A wilted lettuce salad with leaf lettuce substituted for the spinach is also good.

Tomato, Onion and Basil Salad

6   medium size ripe tomatoes
2   medium size yellow onions
    Lettuce leaves for garnish
2   tablespoons basil (4 tablespoons fresh, if available)

Red wine vinegar to taste
Olive oil to taste
Salt and freshly ground black pepper to taste

Select 6 uniform size ripe tomatoes. Make vertical slices at ¼ inch intervals in each tomato, but do not cut quite all the way through the bottoms. Slice onions thinly, (cut larger slices in half). Spread tomato slices slightly and insert an onion slice in each gap. Put a lettuce leaf or two on each salad plate and place a tomato in the center. Still spreading tomato slices slightly, sprinkle generously with basil. Then sprinkle tomatoes generously with red wine vinegar, olive oil, salt and pepper. Let stand a few minutes before serving.

Serves 6.

Tomato Aspic

3	cups tomato juice	2	tablespoons white wine vinegar or lemon juice
½	cup finely chopped celery	1½	teaspoons celery salt
¼	cup finely chopped onion	½	teaspoon sugar
1½	tablespoons Worcestershire sauce	⅛	teaspoon white pepper

Mix foregoing ingredients in a saucepan and simmer 5 minutes.

4	tablespoons unflavored gelatin, (4 envelopes, ¼ ounce each)	½	cup tomato juice

Sprinkle gelatin over ½ cup tomato juice and let stand one minute; then stir into the hot tomato juice mixture. Continue stirring over low heat until gelatin is completely dissolved. Pour mixture into a decorative 2 quart mold (oiled) and put mold in the refrigerator to cool.

2   **ripe tomatoes, peeled, seeded and cut in strips; or ⅓ cup sliced pimento stuffed green olives**

When mixture begins to set (45 minutes to 1 hour), stir in tomatoes or olives and leave in refrigerator for at least 4 hours or overnight.

Unmold the salad on a bed of lettuce and serve with mayonnaise (preferably homemade).

A ring mold with the mayonnaise in a small bowl in the center makes an attractive presentation.

Serves 8 to 10.

Picturesque scene from Paris street market.

Cooked Dressing for Cole Slaw

½	stick margarine or butter		½	teaspoon salt
1	teaspoon flour		1	teaspoon dry mustard
½	cup cider vinegar, heated to boiling		⅛	teaspoon red pepper
¾	cup boiling water		1	teaspoon celery seed
1	tablespoon sugar		3	egg yolks, beaten

In a double boiler over simmering water, melt margarine and whisk in flour. Whisk in vinegar with boiling water, sugar, salt, mustard, red pepper and celery seed. Then gradually whisk in the egg yolks. Continue cooking and whisking until slightly thickened. Cool.

This dressing makes delicious cole slaw with finely shredded fresh cabbage.

Russian Dressing

(1000 Island Dressing)

½	cup mayonnaise		2	tablespoons finely chopped onion
5	tablespoons tomato ketchup		3	tablespoons finely chopped dill pickle relish or dill pickles
2	dashes hot sauce			
½	teaspoon salt		2	tablespoons finely chopped celery
2	tablespoons finely chopped pimento stuffed green olives		1	hard-boiled egg, chopped

All chopped ingredients except egg should be rather fine and excess liquid removed. Mix mayonnaise, ketchup, hot sauce and salt. Then stir in the chopped ingredients, putting the egg in last.

Keeps for a couple of weeks or more in a sealed container in the refrigerator.

Mayonnaise

For most uses, homemade mayonnaise is to be preferred.

Of the commercial varieties, Hellmann's is the best. Even the low calorie Hellmann's is quite good, but the low fat version leaves much to be desired. Hellmann's is sold under the Best Foods label in the West.

3	egg yolks	2	tablespoons lemon juice
1	cup corn, canola or other vegetable oil	1	teaspoon dry mustard
⅓	cup olive oil	1	teaspoon salt
1	tablespoon wine vinegar	⅛	teaspoon red pepper

In a mixmaster or other beater, beat egg yolks thoroughly. Mix vegetable oil and olive oil. Continue beating and add oil, drop by drop at first, then in a small stream. Continue beating and adding oil until all the oil is emulsified. Thin with a little vinegar or lemon juice if mayonnaise begins to thicken too quickly. At the end, while continuing to beat, slowly add remaining vinegar, lemon juice, mustard, salt and pepper.

If the recipe curdles (turns back), stop. Put 2 more egg yolks in a clean bowl. Beat well. Then, while beating, add the curdled mixture a drop at a time at first, then in a small stream. When all of the curdled mixture has been emulsified, add the ingredients remaining from the original recipe.

Adjust the seasoning if necessary.

Makes 1 pint.

Improved Commercial Mayonnaise

This recipe for Improved Mayonnaise is a a lot better than the commercial version and much easier and quicker to make than homemade mayonnaise.

2	cups commercial mayonnaise (preferably Hellmann's)	¼	teaspoon dry mustard
2	tablespoons lemon juice	½	teaspoon salt
1	tablespoon red wine vinegar	⅛	teaspoon white pepper
¼	teaspoon garlic salt	½	cup olive oil

Put mayonnaise in a medium bowl. While whisking or stirring with a large spoon, gradually add lemon juice, vinegar and seasoning. In the same way stir in the olive oil. The dressing should be a little thinner than the original, but will keep its smooth texture.

Makes 2½ cups.

Food Processor Mayonnaise

3	egg yolks	1	tablespoon red wine vinegar
1	egg	½	cup olive oil
¾	teaspoon salt	1½	cups corn, canola or other vegetable oil
2	pinches red pepper	2-3	tablespoons lemon juice
1	teaspoon dry mustard		

Mix olive oil and vegetable oil together. Put egg yolks, egg, salt, cayenne, mustard and vinegar in a food processor fitted with the steel blade. Run machine 5 seconds; without stopping machine, add oil in a fine stream. Mayonnaise should begin to emulsify almost immediately. When well thickened, slowly add the lemon juice.

If mayonnaise does not thicken after some oil has been added, stop. Pour mixture out of food processor, but do not clean. Add 2 more egg yolks to the processor; run for a couple of seconds and begin to add back the old mixture in a fine stream. After old mixture has been emulsified, add rest of oil in a fine stream and then add the lemon juice. Adjust the seasoning if necessary.

Makes 1 pint.

Mayonnaise in a jar with a lid will keep in the refrigerator for 2 weeks or more. The acid in the vinegar or lemon juice keeps it from spoiling.

Mayonnaise Colleé

(Mayonnaise for Masking)

1	teaspoon gelatin	1	cup mayonnaise
2	tablespoons cold water		

Over hot water, dissolve the gelatin in the cold water. Stir it into the mayonnaise.

Mayonnaise colleé is used like frosting to coat cold seafood or various jellied dishes. Using a spatula, apply the mayonnaise colleé with firm strokes. You may decorate the dish with capers, sliced olives, slices of pimento or sliced hard-boiled eggs.

About Oil and Vinegar Dressing

Most mixed green salads are best with a dressing undergirded with olive oil, vinegar, lemon juice, salt and black pepper. I grew up calling this mixture "French Dressing". Today that name has been usurped by a thick, orange, gelatinous mixture that comes in bottles.

"Vinaigrette" was the next name in vogue, but that term suggests chopped onion, pickles and the like.

Today, we refer to "Oil and Vinegar Dressing" for want of a better term. As far as I am concerned, oil means extra virgin olive oil. Based on the requirements of a particular recipe or as a matter of taste, a bland or more pungent olive oil may be selected. But always use top quality oil.

Vinegar ordinarily means white or red wine vinegar - generally white. Again use the best quality. Balsamic vinegar is a relatively new entrant to the salad field and creates a distinctive flavor. Cider vinegar may be used to create a stronger vinegar flavor.

Lemon juice means freshly squeezed juice.

Colman's is the old standby for dry mustard, but other brands do well.

Black pepper means freshly ground black pepper.

While herbs and other condiments may be added, nothing else is required for an exquisite oil and vinegar dressing.

Vegetable stall, Municipal Market, Oxford, England.

Basic Oil and Vinegar Dressing

6	tablespoons extra virgin olive oil	½	teaspoon salt
2	tablespoons lemon juice	¼	teaspoon freshly ground black pepper
2	tablespoons white wine vinegar	1	pinch sugar

Put ingredients in a jar with a lid and shake well before pouring on salad. Dressing keeps well in the refrigerator.

Makes ½ cup.

Variations:

Endless variations are possible. Some examples follow.

Blue Cheese. To 1 cup Basic Oil and Vinegar Dressing, add ¼ cup crumbled blue cheese.

Garlic. To 1 cup Basic Oil and Vinegar Dressing, add 4 cloves garlic peeled and thinly sliced. You may substitute red wine vinegar for white wine vinegar. Let stand several hours before serving.

Fine herbs. To 1 cup Basic Oil and Vinegar Dressing, add 1 tablespoon mixed fine herbs (fresh or dried).

Mustard. To 1 cup Basic Oil and Vinegar Dressing, add 1 teaspoon dry mustard.

Vinegars. Substitute tarragon vinegar in basic recipe or substitute ½ the amount of balsamic vinegar.

Vinaigrette. To 1 cup Basic Oil and Vinegar Dressing (omit the salt), add:

1	tablespoon finely chopped onion	1	tablespoon finely chopped dill or sour pickles
2	tablespoons finely chopped celery		Cayenne pepper
1	tablespoon finely chopped stuffed green olives		

A scant ⅛ teaspoon cayenne pepper may be added to 1 cup dressing in any of these recipes. It adds particular zest to the Blue Cheese recipe.

Seafood

Fresh fish at a supermarket near Santander, Spain.

Seafood

As previously noted, the seafood category is one of my favorites. It seems to lend itself to a greater variety of innovative dishes than most classes of food stuff. It is no accident, therefore, that I have more recipes in this section than any other.

This section includes fish, crab, oysters, scallops, shrimp and a few specialties. It includes hot and cold; poached, steamed, broiled and fried; smoked and pickled; as well as other preparations for seafood.

The simplest and most common ways of cooking seafood are frequently the most difficult to execute with perfection. Fried seafood falls in this category. The method outlined here really works, p.86. As the reader will observe, the fish, scallops or shrimp are alternately dipped in seasoned flour, a milk–egg wash and bread crumbs. The seafood is then plunged in small batches into hot oil (350 to 375 degrees) and cooked until nicely browned. The seafood should be put on paper towels to drain. Served promptly with a good Tartar Sauce, p.88, this fried seafood defies the name. It is crisp, flavorful and not at all greasy!

Another seafood recipe provokes echoes of the past. O'Donnels was a well-known and exceptionally good seafood restaurant in Washington, D.C. Guests were served both at the counter and at tables. Always present on the counter was a big glass jar filled with large Pickled Shrimp, p.105. Adhering to the shrimp still in their shells were all of the spices - celery and mustard seed, bay leaves, red pepper - in which the shrimp had been simmered. As you peeled your shrimp, you could not help but lick your fingers to which these flavorful spices stuck. Served as an appetizer or cold luncheon, these shrimp are without peer.

Fisherman with brace of bright Atlantic salmon, Laxa I Leirasviet, Iceland.

Crabmeat Casserole

(à la Huger)

3   tablespoons finely chopped onion
4   tablespoons butter (divided)
2   tablespoons flour
1   cup milk
¼   cup dry sherry
1   teaspoon horseradish
⅛   teaspoon cayenne pepper (scant)

½   teaspoon salt
¼   teaspoon white pepper
2   teaspoons Worcestershire sauce
1   pound lump crabmeat
4   tablespoons lemon juice
    Buttered bread crumbs

Cook onions in 1 tablespoon butter until limp. Add remaining butter and make a cream sauce with the flour and milk. Stir in sherry, horseradish, cayenne pepper, salt, pepper and Worcestershire sauce.

Sprinkle crabmeat with lemon juice. Gently mix crabmeat and sauce. Pour crabmeat and sauce into a casserole dish. Cover crabmeat with a good layer of crumbs and bake for 30 minutes in a preheated 350 degree oven. Raise heat the last few minutes if needed to brown crumbs.

Serves 4.

Jamaican curb market in the early 1960's.

Crab Cakes

1   pound lump crabmeat
1   cup soft white bread crumbs
6   tablespoons finely chopped onion
     (or green onions)
4   tablespoons finely chopped green pepper
6   tablespoons chopped fresh parsley
4   tablespoons lemon juice
2   tablespoons mayonnaise
2   eggs, slightly beaten

1   tablespoon dry mustard
1½   tablespoons Worcestershire sauce
4   dashes hot sauce
½   teaspoon salt
¼   teaspoon black pepper
     Fine cracker crumbs
     Vegetable oil for frying
     Lemon wedges for garnish

Jumbo lump crabmeat is too large, but you do want lump. Break up any large lumps or reserve them for another use. With two spoons mix crabmeat, soft bread crumbs, onion, green pepper, parsley, lemon juice and mayonnaise.

Beat eggs, stir in mustard, Worcestershire sauce, hot sauce and salt and pepper. Combine lightly with crabmeat mixture.

Plop a handful of crabmeat mixture on cracker crumbs; form into a cake about ¾ inch thick and 2½ inches in diameter. Pat crumbs on top and sides of cakes (handle gently with hands and spatula).

Put about ½ inch vegetable oil in a skillet and heat over medium heat. With a spatula, slide crab cakes into the oil and brown on one side; turn and brown the other. Drain on absorbent paper.

Serve crab cakes with lemon wedges. Tartar Sauce, p.88, is optional.

Serves 6.

Deviled Crab

1	stick butter, melted		1	teaspoon dry mustard
3	tablespoons finely chopped onion		½	teaspoon salt
½	cup chopped celery		¼	teaspoon black pepper
1	tablespoon chopped parsley		1	cup soft bread crumbs
1	tablespoon Worcestershire sauce		1	egg
2	tablespoons lemon juice		1	pound lump crabmeat
4	dashes hot sauce			Buttered cracker crumbs

In a sauté pan, mix all ingredients except egg, crabmeat and cracker crumbs. Simmer over low heat for 8 to 10 minutes. Stir the beaten egg into the crabmeat and stir mixture into the sauté pan. When heated, pile crabmeat mixture into scallop shells*, top with crumbs and bake in a preheated 400 degree oven until browned on top (about 15 minutes).

*If you do not want to use individual scallop shells, pour crab mixture into a casserole dish and cover with crumbs.

Serves 6.

Municipal fish market, San Sebastian, Spain.

Crabmeat Mornay

2	cups Cream Sauce	¾	teaspoon salt
2	egg yolks	4	tablespoons dry sherry
4	dashes cayenne	1½	tablespoons butter
½	teaspoon dry mustard	2½	tablespoons finely chopped onion
4	tablespoons grated and slightly packed Cheddar or Swiss cheese	1	pound lump crabmeat
1	tablespoon chopped parsley		Buttered bread crumbs and grated Parmesan cheese to cover
⅛	teaspoon ground nutmeg		

Make Cream Sauce, p.115, and beat in egg yolks. Stir in cayenne, mustard, cheese, parsley, nutmeg, salt and sherry. In a sauté pan melt butter and sauté onions until limp. Add crabmeat and stir until warm. Handle gently so as not to break up lumps of crabmeat. Add cream sauce. Heat and blend.

Turn mixture into a shallow baking dish; sprinkle with buttered crumbs and Parmesan cheese.

Bake in a preheated 400 degree oven until lightly browned and bubbly (12 to 15 minutes).

Serves 5 to 6.

Crabmeat and Bacon Sandwich

(The Cloister, Sea Island, Georgia)

⅓	cup fresh lump crabmeat	2-3	lettuce leaves
2	tablespoons finely chopped celery	2	slices white or multi-grain bread
1	tablespoon finely chopped onion		Salt
3	tablespoons mayonnaise (divided)		Black pepper
3	slices crisp bacon		

Mix crabmeat, celery, onion and 2 tablespoons mayonnaise. Toast white or multi-grain bread according to taste. Spread one slice of toast with crabmeat mixture and top with bacon slices and lettuce leaves. Spread other slice of toast with remaining mayonnaise; sprinkle with salt and pepper to taste; and put on top of sandwich. Slice in half diagonally and serve.

Crabmeat Ravigote

2 cups lump crabmeat

4 tablespoons white wine vinegar

4 tablespoons chopped chives (or 6 tablespoons finely chopped onion)

1 cup mayonnaise

2 hard-boiled eggs, finely grated

4 tablespoons capers

Salt and white pepper to taste

Moisten crabmeat with the vinegar and drain well. Combine crabmeat with chives and mayonnaise. Season with salt and pepper to taste. Mound crabmeat mixture in scallop shells and spread with mayonnaise, then grated hard-boiled egg and dot with capers.

If you do not want to use scallop shells mound crabmeat mixture on a serving plate and cover with mayonnaise, hard-boiled egg and capers.

Chill and serve.

Serves 4.

For a Creole Touch Add to Mayonnaise

3 teaspoons dry mustard

3 teaspoons prepared horseradish

2 tablespoons minced parsley

Use pimento strips for garnish.

Stuffed Soft-Shell Crabs

8	soft shell crabs		Salt
½	pound lump crabmeat		Black pepper
1	egg	1	stick butter
	Flour	4	lemon wedges

Clean soft shell crabs. Lift back covers of crabs and stuff each crab with about 1½ tablespoons lump crabmeat. Replace back covers. Beat egg and dilute it with ¾ cup water. Dip crabs in egg mixture and dust with flour seasoned with salt and pepper.

Melt butter in a large iron skillet and sauté crabs quickly until nicely browned on each side. (May be necessary to cook crabs in two batches.) Drain crabs on absorbent paper and serve with lemon wedges and Tartar Sauce, p.88.

Serves 4.

Fisherman's Catch

1	pound bay scallops	¼	teaspoon black pepper
1	pound boiled shrimp, shelled	3	cups milk
1	pound lump crabmeat	3	tablespoons chopped parsley
1	stick butter	3	tablespoons Worcestershire sauce
8	tablespoons flour	6	tablespoons lemon juice
¾	teaspoon salt	1	cup buttered bread crumbs

Put scallops in a colander and pour 1 kettle boiling water over them. Drain. In a medium sauté pan melt butter over low heat and whisk in flour, salt and pepper. Add milk slowly while whisking rapidly to avoid lumps. When heated, but not boiling, stir in parsley, Worcestershire sauce and lemon juice.

In a large bowl, mix scallops, shrimp and crabmeat. Then pour in sauce. Mix well. Pour mixture into a buttered 3 quart casserole dish. Top with bread crumbs. Bake in a preheated 350 degree oven 30 to 40 minutes or until hot and bubbly.

Serve over long grain white rice.

Serves 8 to 10.

Fish Fillets with Lump Crabmeat Sauce

(Galatoires, New Orleans)

For the Fish

4-6	fish fillets, skin removed		¼	teaspoon white pepper
1	cup flour			Pinch paprika
¼	teaspoon salt		4	tablespoons butter

Each fillet should be large enough for one serving. This recipe was designed for sea trout which is not always available in fish markets. Flounder, sea bass or other salt water fish that is not too coarse substitute well.

Rinse fillets and pat dry. On a plate mix flour, salt, white pepper and paprika. Dredge fillets in the seasoned flour and shake off excess. Melt 4 tablespoons butter in a large skillet over medium high heat. Sauté fillets until golden on both sides (1 to 2 minutes per side). Keep warm.

Sauce

6	tablespoons butter		½	pound lump crabmeat
2	teaspoons red or white wine vinegar		2	tablespoons chopped parsley
2	teaspoons lemon juice			Lemon wedges and parsley for garnish

While fillets are cooking, melt 6 tablespoons butter in a saucepan. Continue cooking over medium low heat, whisking occasionally, until butter turns golden-brown. Combine vinegar and lemon juice and gradually whisk into the butter. Add crabmeat and parsley to the butter. Mix and heat through. Keep warm.

Put fish fillets on platter or individual plates. Spoon crabmeat and sauce over fillets. Garnish with lemon wedges and parsley.

Serves 4 to 6.

About Deep Frying

Deep frying means that the ingredients are cooked in oil that is at least 3 inches deep and ordinarily deeper. Almost by definition, some dishes must be deep fried. French fried potatoes and hush puppies are examples.

Red mullet, Basque Coast, Spain.

In deep frying, the ingredients are plunged into hot oil and quickly sealed on the outsides while the insides are actually steamed by the moisture in the ingredients. To accomplish this result with the ingredients nicely browned on the outside at the same time that the insides are cooked through, the oil must be at a proper temperature. In addition, the size of a batch to be cooked at one time must be relatively small so that the temperature of the oil is not reduced too much when the ingredients are added.

For deep frying the beginning temperature of the oil should be between 350 and 375 degrees. Besides using a thermometer there are several ways to determine the correct temperature. Cook books refer to "hot but not smoking". At the proper temperature, a ½ inch cube of bread will brown in about 1 minute. An old fashioned way to signal the correct temperature was to float a kitchen match in the oil. The match would burst into flame when the oil reached the proper temperature. Finally trial and error with small initial batches always works.

To repeat the fundamentals, have your oil at the proper temperature and cook in small batches. Adjust the heat depending on the early results.

Fried Fish

1	cup flour	8	dashes hot sauce	
1	teaspoon salt	1	cup fine bread crumbs	
½	teaspoon black pepper	2	pounds fish fillets, skin removed	
1	egg		Vegetable oil for frying	
1	cup milk		Lemon quarters, for garnish	

Use Three Bowls

Bowl one: mix flour, salt and pepper.

Bowl two: beat egg and stir in milk and hot sauce.

Bowl three: bread crumbs.

Dredge fish fillets in flour, then milk mixture and then bread crumbs. Shake off excess crumbs.

In an iron skillet, heat enough vegetable oil to just cover the fillets until hot but not smoking (about 375 degrees).

Fry fish fillets in one layer until nicely browned. You may want to turn fillets for the last couple of minutes so that tops will be evenly browned.

Serve with lemon quarters and Tartar Sauce, p.88.

Sea trout, sea bass, flounder, perch and catfish are among the fish that fry well.

This specific frying technique came from the West Texas Ranch of my good friend, Brien Dillon.

Tartar Sauce

2	tablespoons finely chopped onion	1	tablespoon finely chopped dill pickle or 1 tablespoon India relish (drained)
2	tablespoons finely chopped pimento stuffed green olives	1	tablespoon finely chopped capers
		1	cup mayonnaise

Mix chopped ingredients with the mayonnaise.

For an extra touch, you may add 1 tablespoon finely chopped fresh parsley.

The flavors in tartar sauce blend better if kept in refrigerator for a few hours before using. Sauce will keep in a sealed container in refrigerator for 2 to 3 weeks.

Tartar sauce is one of the few recipes in which commercial mayonnaise works as well or better than homemade. I recommend Improved Commercial Mayonnaise, p.72.

Green Giardiniera Sauce

(For Broiled or Sautéed Fish)

1	cup Giardiniera pickled vegetables*	1	tablespoon capers
½	cup chopped fresh basil leaves (lightly packed)	6	tablespoons olive oil
		3	tablespoons balsamic vinegar
¼	cup chopped fresh parsley (lightly packed)	½	teaspoon salt
2	tablespoons chopped onion	⅛	teaspoon black pepper

Put pickled vegetables in a food processor fitted with the steel blade and process until smooth. Add basil leaves, parsley, onion and capers and continue processing until well blended. Add olive oil, vinegar, salt and black pepper and process into a thick sauce.

This sauce has an unusual sharp taste that goes well with broiled or sautéed salt water fish.

*Giardiniera pickled vegetables are imported and found at most fine food stores. Krinos is a familiar brand.

Oyster Fritters

2	eggs	¾	teaspoon salt
¼	cup milk	⅓	teaspoon black pepper
4	tablespoons finely chopped onion	8	ounces oysters
1	cup flour		Vegetable oil for frying
1¼	teaspoons baking powder		

Beat eggs; add milk; stir in onion, flour, baking powder, salt and pepper. Chop oysters medium fine (should have 1½ to 2 cups). Add oysters to batter with enough oyster liquid to make a thick batter.

Drop batter by tablespoon in deep hot oil. Fry until nicely browned (about 1½ minutes on each side). Drain fritters on absorbent paper. Sprinkle with salt. Serve hot.

If you like, you can add to batter 2 tablespoons chopped parsley and 2 tablespoons finely chopped celery. For lighter fritters, beat egg whites separately and fold into batter.

Scalloped Oysters

¾	stick butter, melted	4-6	dashes hot sauce
2	tablespoons finely chopped onion	½	teaspoon ground nutmeg
1½	sleeves of saltines, coarsely crumbled		Salt and black pepper to taste
1	quart fresh oysters in their liquid	1	cup cream

Butter a shallow casserole dish. In a sauté pan melt the remaining butter and sauté the onions until limp. In the bottom of the casserole dish put a ½ inch layer of crumbled saltines; and top with the oysters. Pour the melted butter and onions over the oysters; season with hot sauce, nutmeg and salt and pepper to taste. Pour cream over all and top with another ½ inch layer of crumbled saltines. Bake immediately in a preheated 350 degree oven for about 45 to 50 minutes until nicely browned and bubbly.

Scalloped oysters are delicious with roast stuffed turkey on Thanksgiving or Christmas Day.

Serves 6 to 8.

Oyster Stew

(Gongie's Recipe)

6	tablespoons butter	2	tablespoons chopped parsley
1	tablespoon finely chopped onion	⅛	teaspoon paprika
1	pint oysters		Salt and black pepper to taste
6	cloves	3	cups half-and-half
3	dashes hot sauce		Butter to taste
1	tablespoon Worcestershire sauce		Paprika for garnish
½	teaspoon celery salt		Chopped parsley to taste

Melt butter and sauté onions until clear. Add oysters and cloves, hot sauce, Worcestershire sauce, celery salt, parsley, paprika and salt and pepper to taste. Simmer for a couple of minutes. Then add half-and-half and bring rapidly to a boil. Dot with butter and sprinkle with paprika and parsley. Serve at once.

Serves 2 to 3.

About Poached Fish

A fish poacher fitted with a poaching rack is the ideal container for poaching fish. A roasting pan, however, makes a good substitute. It is a good idea to put the fish in the poacher ahead of time and determine the amount of liquid needed to cover it. The fish holds together better if wrapped in a couple of thicknesses of cheesecloth, but this step is not essential.

Measure the thickness of fish at the thickest part of its body and simmer exactly 10 minutes per inch of thickness.

Make enough Court-Bouillon, p.92, to cover the fish. Over two stove eyes, bring the Bouillon to a boil. Carefully lower fish into the simmering Bouillon. Cover fish poacher and bring liquid back to a simmer. After liquid has returned to a simmer, start timing. Do not allow liquid to boil while fish is immersed as boiling may cause fish to be tough and flesh to break up. When time is up, remove fish from the liquid and drain immediately.

School of fish photographed through a glass bottom boat, Great Barrier Reef, Australia.

Court-Bouillon

(For Fish)

1½ gallons water	12 sprigs parsley
3 medium onions, cut in half	24 whole black peppercorns
6 whole cloves	1 lemon, sliced
3 bay leaves	3 tablespoons salt
Green tops from 1 stalk celery	

Put one clove in each onion half. Combine ingredients in a stock pot and simmer 15 minutes.

For a special court-bouillon, you may substitute one bottle of dry white wine for 1 quart of water.

This recipe makes enough court-bouillon to poach a large salmon or other big fish.

Poached Salmon

1   **whole salmon or chunk of salmon**

The best way to cook a whole salmon is by poaching. The maximum size of the fish is limited by the size of your fish poacher. A 5 to 6 pound salmon does well. If you do not need a whole salmon, buy a section of the fish. In either event do not skin the fish, and I prefer not to remove the head or tail.

Make enough Court-Bouillon, above, to cover the salmon and follow the instructions for Poaching Fish, p.91. As soon as fish is cooked and drained, skin one side of fish; remove fins and scrape off dark oily meat. Turn fish gently and skin and scrape the other side. If cheesecloth was used, turning is easier.

If fish is to be served hot, arrange fish on a platter with parsley. Accompany the fish with Hollandaise Sauce, p.182, and lemon wedges.

If fish is to be served cold, cover top side with Mayonnaise Colleé, p.73. Garnish the salmon with sliced cucumbers, hard-boiled egg quarters and parsley sprigs or fresh dill. Mayonnaise may be substituted for the Mayonnaise Colleé, but it does not hold up as well.

Cured Salmon

(Charcoal Broiled with Dill)

2   pounds fresh salmon fillets, skinned (2 center cut pieces)

¾   cup sugar

¼   cup coarse salt

1   tablespoon white peppercorns, coarsely crushed

1   large bunch (about 2 ounces) dill, coarsely chopped

Cured salmon is a great party dish because most of the preparation is done ahead of time.

Wipe fillets with damp cloth and remove any bones.

Combine sugar, salt and pepper.

Put one third of the sugar, salt, pepper and dill on a piece of plastic wrap. Lay one salmon fillet on top of this mixture. Put another third of the mixture on top of the salmon fillet. Top with the second salmon fillet and spread the final third of the mixture over the second salmon fillet. Wrap tightly in plastic wrap. Weight the salmon down with cutting boards, bricks, jugs of milk, whatever. Marinate in the refrigerator for 36 to 48 hours, turning every 12 hours. Remove salmon from the refrigerator and scrape off mixture. Grill over hot coals until just done through (about 5 minutes per side).

Garnish with dill sprigs or edible flowers.

Serves 4.

A Buenos Aires fish market.

Sautéed Salmon Fillets

The Malleo, as well as the Collon Cura, Chimehuin and other Argentine rivers are among the premier trout streams in the world. There, rainbow and brown trout challenge flyfishers from many distant countries.

2	tablespoons butter	Salt
2	tablespoons olive oil	Black pepper
2	pounds salmon fillets	Juice of ½ lemon
	(skin removed from both sides)	Lemon wedges for garnish
	Flour	

Select salmon fillets that are between ¾ and 1¼ inches thick. In a sauté pan or skillet over medium heat, melt butter and stir in olive oil. Dust salmon fillets in flour seasoned with salt and pepper and shake off the excess. Sauté fillets over medium heat, turning once until nicely browned on both sides and opaque in the center (time varies according to the thickness of the fillets, but 5 minutes per side is typical).

Squeeze ½ lemon over fillets after they have been turned and serve with lemon wedges. Pour browned butter and olive oil over fillets.

Serves 6.

As a variation, chop 2 hard-boiled eggs medium and swirl into butter and oil before pouring over the salmon; or do the same with 2 tablespoons capers; or use both.

Charbroiled Atlantic Salmon

(Bob Izard)

½   cup soy sauce

¼   cup olive oil

2   teaspoons powdered ginger

½   Atlantic salmon fillet (skin on, but backbone removed - 3 to 4 pounds)

Lemon wedges for garnish

Mix soy sauce, olive oil and ginger. Put sauce in a gallon baggie. Fold salmon and put in baggie and marinate 1 to 2 hours. Shake a couple of times.

Prepare a hot bed of charcoal and grill salmon skin side down for about 4 to 5 minutes. Salmon should be about 3 inches from the coals. Turn salmon; peel off skin; and broil for another 4 to 5 minutes.

Salmon should be nicely browned on meat side.

Serve with lemon wedges.

Serves 6.

Our son, Bailey, with a large brown trout from the Yellowstone River, Montana.

Creamed Scallops with Fresh Dill

1 pound bay scallops; or sea scallops, cut in halves or thirds if large

1 cup dry white wine

2 bay leaves

12 black peppercorns

3 sprigs parsley

Put the foregoing ingredients in a saucepan with enough water to just cover the scallops. Bring to a boil and simmer 3 to 5 minutes until scallops are just cooked through.

4 tablespoons finely chopped shallots

4 tablespoons butter

3 tablespoons flour

2 cups half-and-half

⅓ cup snipped fresh dill (about ⅜ inches long), lightly packed

1 teaspoon salt

White pepper to taste

4 lemon wedges

Sauté shallots in butter until limp. Stir in flour and whisk roux until well blended. Slowly add half-and-half, whisking constantly, and continue to cook over low heat until the sauce is nicely thickened. Add salt and pepper to taste and fresh dill. Stir in scallops and, if sauce is too thick, a little of the poaching liquid. Correct seasoning and serve with lemon wedges.

Fresh dill is the essential ingredient for this recipe.

Serves 4.

An option is to slice 6 ounces fresh mushrooms, sauté them in a little butter and add them to the cream sauce with the scallops.

Savory Scallops

3   tablespoons olive oil (divided)

4   medium shallots, finely chopped
       (about ⅓ cup)

3   large tomatoes, peeled, seeded and
       chopped (about 2 cups)

⅔   cup dry white wine

1   tablespoon chopped fresh basil

½   tablespoon chopped fresh rosemary

1   tablespoon chopped fresh parsley

3   cloves garlic, minced

2   pounds sea scallops

¼   teaspoon salt

¼   teaspoon black pepper

      Lemon wedges for garnish

Heat 2 tablespoons olive oil over medium heat. Add shallots and sauté until limp (about 3 minutes). Add tomatoes, wine, basil, rosemary, parsley, garlic, salt and pepper. Simmer 8 to 10 minutes or until slightly reduced.

Sear scallops, following the instructions for Seared Scallops, below. Spoon scallops onto a serving plate; pour sauce over them; and garnish with parsley.

Serves 6.

Seared Scallops

1   pound sea scallops
       (preferable about ½ inch thick)

      Olive oil

      Lemon wedges

If scallops are too thick, slice them in half horizontally. Heat a cast iron skillet until extremely hot. Cover skillet with a thin coating of olive oil and add scallops in a single layer. Sear until nicely browned (about 1½ minutes); turn and brown the other side. Adjust heat so that scallops just loose their translucent look in the center when they are browned on both sides. Try a couple of sample scallops at first. Do not overcook or scallops will become tough.

Serve with lemon wedges and Tartar Sauce, p.88.

Serves 3 to 4.

Scallops with Tomatoes and Bacon

6	strips bacon	½	cup finely chopped onion
6	toast rounds (3 to 4 inches in diameter)	1	cup finely diced fresh tomatoes
	Olive oil for frying (divided)	3	tablespoons chopped chives
1	pound sea scallops		Salt and black pepper to taste

Fry bacon until crisp. Toast bread rounds.

In a very hot skillet just coated with olive oil, quickly sauté scallops until lightly browned on both sides (slice thick scallops in ½ inch rounds). Remove scallops and keep warm.

While scallops are cooking, put a little olive oil in another pan and sauté onion until limp. Then spread about 2 teaspoons onion on each toast. Cover onion with a layer of scallops. Quickly warm tomatoes in scallop pan and put 1 tablespoon tomatoes on each toast. Sprinkle with chives and salt and pepper, to taste; top with a strip of bacon broken in two pieces; and drizzle with warm Basic Oil and Vinegar Dressing, p.75.

Serves 4 to 6.

A bright fall accent, Ponoi River, Russia.

Fresh Shad Roe

2	pairs fresh shad roe	1	tablespoon Worcestershire sauce
1	stick butter	2	tablespoons chopped parsley
	Flour for dusting	4	toast points
	Salt and black pepper to taste	4	slices crisp bacon for garnish
	Juice of ½ lemon		Lemon wedges for garnish

Select a skillet that will just hold the shad roe in a single layer. Melt butter over medium heat (butter should be ¼ to ½ inch deep). Dust shad roe with flour seasoned with salt and pepper. Sauté in butter, covered, over low heat - about 10 minutes per side. Toward end, sprinkle with lemon juice and Worcestershire sauce.

Just before removing from skillet, sprinkle shad roe with parsley. Serve on toast points, with crisp bacon slices and lemon wedges.

Canned shad roe is also very good and can be prepared the same way. It takes less cooking time, however, since it is precooked.

Serves 3 to 4.

Fresh shad roe is not found regularly in the markets, but shows up in the spring when shad are running in our Southeastern and Eastern rivers. Fresh shad roe should be sautéed over low heat until cooked through and nicely browned. Canned shad roe is also a delicacy.

Barbecued Shrimp

Serve barbecued shrimp with heated French bread for dipping and a green salad. Also provide a couple of refuse bowls for the shrimp shells and plenty of paper napkins or towels.

1½	sticks butter		1	lemon, sliced
1½	sticks margarine		2	teaspoons crumbled rosemary
1	tablespoon black pepper (finely ground)		1	teaspoon crumbled oregano
6	dashes hot sauce		1	teaspoon salt
5	tablespoons Worcestershire sauce		⅓	cup red wine vinegar
2	cloves garlic, sliced		4	pounds unpeeled large shrimp (about 32 count)
	Juice of 1 lemon			

Melt butter and margarine, mix in all other ingredients except shrimp. In this mixture marinate shrimp 2 to 4 hours. Recipe works, however, even if you do not have time to marinate the shrimp. Incidentally, 1 tablespoon is the correct amount of black pepper. Baking reduces the heat of the pepper, but leaves its flavor.

Put shrimp and marinade in a large roasting pan so that shrimp are not more than two layers deep. Bake uncovered in a preheated 400 degree oven for about 20 minutes. Turn shrimp a couple of times. Do not overcook.

Ladle shrimp and sauce into individual bowls.

Serves 12.

Breakfast Shrimp

(Charleston, S.C.)

4	slices bacon	2	teaspoons Worcestershire sauce
1	pound small raw shrimp, peeled (60 to 70 count shrimp are ideal)	1	tablespoon tomato ketchup
4	tablespoons finely chopped onion	¼	teaspoon salt
2	tablespoons finely chopped green bell pepper	⅛	teaspoon black pepper
		2	dashes hot sauce
		2	tablespoons flour

In a sauté pan over medium heat, fry bacon until crisp. Set bacon aside. In the bacon drippings (should have about 3 tablespoons), sauté onion and green pepper until onion is golden. Add shrimp and turn several times in bacon grease. Pour in about one cup water and simmer 2 to 3 minutes (water should not totally cover shrimp). Add remaining ingredients except flour and mix. Stir flour into a little warm water and then stir into the shrimp mixture. Continue to simmer for 2 to 3 minutes until sauce thickens. Crumble reserved bacon, stir bacon into shrimp and serve.

Grits are essential with this breakfast dish.

Serves 6.

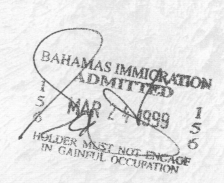

Broiled Shrimp
(Mexican Style)

6 strips bacon

1 medium onion

1 green bell pepper

1 pound large shrimp, peeled and deveined

Cut bacon in 1 inch lengths. Peel onion, cut in eighths and separate sections. Remove ribs and seeds from green pepper and cut in eighths.

On skewers, alternate, bacon pieces, onion sections, green pepper and shrimp. (Thread shrimp in crescent shapes through front and tail.)

Sauce

2 sticks butter

6 cloves garlic, minced

Juice of 1 lemon

½ teaspoon salt

¼ teaspoon black pepper

In a small saucepan, melt butter and sauté garlic until it takes on a little color. Add lemon juice, salt and pepper.

After skewers have been filled, brush with sauce and cook over charcoal until lightly browned, basting occasionally with more sauce. Serve with extra sauce and heated French bread.

Curried Shrimp

1½	pounds shrimp
2	tablespoons olive oil
1	cup chopped onion
½	cup chopped bell pepper
2	cloves garlic, sliced
2	tablespoons flour
1½-2	cups beef broth
½	cup chopped celery

1	cup tomatoes, peeled, seeded and chopped
2	tablespoons chopped parsley
1	bay leaf
1½	tablespoons soy sauce
1-1½	tablespoons medium curry powder
1	tablespoon chutney
½	teaspoon salt

The original recipe suggests that the curried shrimp be garnished with fried banana slices. More conventional side dishes might include crumbled crisp bacon, chopped hard-boiled egg, chopped onion and chopped chutney.

Plunge shrimp in boiling water and return water to a boil. Cook 2 minutes. Pour shrimp into a colander, cool with running water, peel and devein.

Put olive oil in large frying pan with onion, bell pepper and garlic. Sauté until vegetables are limp: sprinkle with flour and combine. Slowly stir in 1 cup beef broth. Add celery, tomatoes, parsley, bay leaf, soy sauce, curry powder, chutney and salt. Simmer 20 minutes stirring occasionally. Add more beef broth, if needed. Add shrimp, heat through and serve on white rice.

Serves 8.

Colorful fresh shrimp, Paris street market.

Shrimp de Jonghe

1	pound shrimp		Salt and red pepper to taste
½	stick butter	4	tablespoons finely chopped parsley
2	cloves garlic, thinly sliced	3	tablespoons lemon juice

Put shrimp in rapidly boiling water and cook for 2 minutes. Pour shrimp in a colander, cool, peel and devein.

In a sauté pan, brown garlic in butter and discard garlic. Add boiled shrimp and brown lightly on both sides (5 to 10 minutes in all). Sprinkle shrimp lightly with salt and red pepper. Add parsley and toss well. At the last minute, add the lemon juice. Accompany Shrimp de Jonghe with white rice.

Serves 4.

Shrimp Étouffée

1	medium onion, finely chopped	1	tablespoon Worcestershire sauce
2	green onions, finely chopped	4	dashes hot sauce
3-4	cloves garlic, minced	1	teaspoon salt
¼	cup finely chopped celery	½	teaspoon sugar
½	cup butter	½	teaspoon thyme
2	tablespoons flour	⅛	teaspoon black pepper
2½	cups water	1	pound shrimp, peeled (nearly 2 pounds in shell)
1	can tomato purée (10½ ounce)		
2	bay leaves	2	eggs, hard-boiled and quartered

Sauté onion, green onions, garlic and celery in butter until tender. Add flour; cook and stir until lightly browned. Add remaining ingredients, except shrimp and eggs; blend well and simmer uncovered, stirring occasionally, 25 minutes, or until almost the desired consistency. Add shrimp; cook 15 minutes longer. Transfer to a serving dish and garnish with the eggs. Serve with white rice.

Serves 6 to 8.

Marinated Shrimp

2   pounds large shrimp, boiled and peeled
1   cup thinly sliced onion (slices cut in half)

2   cups celery, cut in bite size chunks

Marinade

¼   cup tarragon vinegar
¾   cup olive oil
¼   cup lemon juice
3   lemons, sliced
1   tablespoon Worcestershire sauce
1   tablespoon mushroom sauce*

1   tablespoon salt
1   teaspoon whole black peppercorns
4   bay leaves
1   teaspoon sugar
2   tablespoons capers
1   teaspoon paprika

Mix marinade.

Put shrimp, onion and celery in the marinade and mix well. Let stand in refrigerator for several hours or overnight. Stir once or twice.

If mushroom sauce is not available, substitute A-1 Steak Sauce or omit.

Serves 10 to 12.

Pickled Shrimp

(O'Donnels, Washington, D.C.)

1   cup vinegar
1   cup beer (or water)
2   tablespoons celery seed
2   teaspoons mustard seed

2   teaspoons coarse ground black pepper
½   teaspoon crushed red pepper
2   teaspoons salt
1   pound large shrimp

Bring liquids and seasoning to a boil. Add shrimp and boil gently for about 4 minutes. Cool in the liquid. Then drain shrimp in a colander, letting seasoning adhere to the shrimp.

Let guests peel their own shrimp - hot or at room temperature.

Pickled shrimp are excellent for lunch or as an appetizer.

Serves 4 to 6.

Scampi

(Hana Maui)

12 ounces white wine	Juice of ½ lemon
3 tablespoons crushed capers	3 tablespoons chopped parsley
1 stick butter	Paprika, to taste
3 garlic cloves, crushed	1 pound jumbo shrimp, peeled and deveined, leaving tails
1 tablespoon Worcestershire sauce	

In a saucepan over medium heat, simmer white wine and capers until reduced to one quarter, set aside.

In a sauté pan over medium heat, melt butter and mix in garlic, Worcestershire sauce and lemon juice. After a couple of minutes, stir in reserved wine, capers and chopped parsley.

Arrange shrimp in an oven proof pan large enough to hold shrimp in one layer; spoon butter sauce over shrimp; and sprinkle with paprika.

The sauce should half cover the shrimp. Bake shrimp in a preheated 450 degree oven 8 to 12 minutes depending on size of shrimp. Shrimp should be browned on top and cooked through.

Serve at once over rice or pasta.

Serves 4 to 6.

Shrimp in Tomato-Feta Cheese Sauce

(Athens, Greece)

6	tablespoons olive oil	1	teaspoon salt
1	cup coarsely chopped onion	1	teaspoon freshly ground black pepper
4	large cloves garlic, minced	1	teaspoon sugar
½	cup chopped celery with some leaves	½	cup tomato paste
3	cups ripe tomatoes, peeled, seeded and chopped (1½ to 2 pounds)	2	teaspoons dill weed
2	tablespoons shredded fresh basil or 1½ tablespoons dried	2	tablespoons lemon juice
		½	cup crumbled feta cheese
		1½	pounds large shrimp, boiled and peeled

Heat the olive oil in a large sauté pan over medium heat. Sauté the onion, garlic and celery, stirring occasionally, until limp (5 to 8 minutes). Add the tomatoes, basil, salt, pepper and sugar and simmer uncovered over medium heat for 30 minutes.

Add the tomato paste, dill weed and lemon juice and simmer 10 minutes longer. Add a little more water if needed. Stir in feta cheese; then add shrimp. Continue cooking until shrimp are just heated through.

Serves 8.

You may substitute 30 ounces peeled Italian plum tomatoes for the ripe tomatoes.

Red Snapper Vera Cruz

4	snapper fillets (skinned) (about 1½ pounds)		3	cups tomatoes, seeded and chopped (about 12 medium plum tomatoes)
	Flour for dusting		2	tablespoons capers
	Salt and black pepper to taste		6	tablespoons chopped fresh cilantro
½	cup olive oil (divided)		¼	teaspoon cinnamon
6	garlic cloves, sliced thin		¼	teaspoon ground cloves
1	medium onion, sliced thin		¾	cup sliced green, pimento stuffed olives
2	jalapeño peppers, cut in fine strips			Salt and black pepper to taste
				Juice of 1 lime

Flounder, mahi-mahi or other fine grained salt water fish may be used instead of snapper. Dust fillets lightly with flour seasoned with salt and pepper.

Heat ½ olive oil in skillet and cook fillets until they are browned on both sides and flake easily. Remove fillets and keep warm.

Add rest of olive oil, garlic, onion and jalapeño pepper to the skillet. When the vegetables are soft, add tomatoes, capers, cilantro, cinnamon, cloves and salt and pepper to taste. Return fish to pan, sprinkle with lime juice and heat everything together.

Serves 4.

Fillets of Sole Meunière

6   fillets of sole or flounder
    Flour for dredging
    Salt and black pepper to taste
3   tablespoons butter (divided)

1½ tablespoons vegetable oil
    Juice of ½ lemon
2   tablespoons chopped parsley

Wash fillets, blot, and dredge in flour well seasoned with salt and pepper. Shake off excess flour. In a large skillet heat 1½ tablespoons butter and vegetable oil. Over medium high heat sauté the fillets on one side until nicely browned. Turn and brown the other side. Just before fillets are done, add some extra butter, the lemon juice and parsley. Pour the sauce over the fillets and serve.

Garnish with lemon wedges.

Dover Sole is the classic for this recipe, but fillets from any type of small flounder work well.

Serves 6.

Charbroiled Swordfish Steaks

(Bob Izard)

5   tablespoons olive oil
¼   cup Dijon style mustard

4   swordfish steaks (cut ½ to ¾ inch thick)
    Lemon wedges for garnish

Prepare a hot charcoal fire.

Gradually work olive oil into the mustard until well combined. Spread mustard-olive oil mixture on one side of swordfish steaks and put on grill mustard side down. Steaks should be about 3 inches from the coals. Broil steaks until well browned and crusted (about 7 minutes). Brush top sides of steaks with mustard mixture and turn. Broil 5 minutes longer.

Remove steaks to a hot platter and serve with lemon wedges.

Tartar Sauce, p.88, is an excellent accompaniment to this recipe. You may want to dilute the tartar sauce with a little extra mayonnaise.

Serves 6.

Poultry & Game

Free-range chickens along the road
in a small Chinese village near
the Yangt ze River, China.

Poultry and Game Birds

This section covers chickens, turkeys, ducks and their wild predecessors. Besides the obvious genealogical relationship between the two categories, there are important trends affecting both. Over the last few decades, the poultry industry has manipulated genetics to produce larger and faster growing birds, has used ever more confined pens and has provided artificial light to keep the birds feeding 24 hours a day. The sole quest is to transform feed grain into poultry in the most efficient manner. It is small wonder that the feed grain companies control most of the poultry industry.

More efficient production has its costs. The poultry looses both texture and flavor. The encouraging trend is that free range chickens, see picture, p.110, are once again available in many fine markets. Hopefully this trend will accelerate.

On the wild side, the spread of real estate development and continued pressure from hunters have decreased populations of wild birds. To replace them, game birds are being raised in captivity. These birds are a welcome addition to the table. When released in the wild, however, these birds are poor substitutes for the real thing. This practice is depriving a new generation of the challenge and thrill of hunting truly wild game. Again, however, there are hopeful trends. Conservation efforts, as well as scientific research, are leading to the restoration of wild stocks. Ducks Unlimited's success with water fowl is a testament to habitat improvement. In Georgia, Tall Timbers and the Auburn Project are making strides to unravel the complicated web that affects increased quail populations.

But, back to cooking. This section has a number of excellent poultry recipes, but its real strength is wild quail, doves, duck and turkey. I have enjoyed bird hunting for more than 60 years. Included are a number of recipes from the South and a few from Mexico and elsewhere. Now that game is available in the market, these recipes are worth trying even if you do not have a hunter in the family.

Creamed Chicken or Turkey

4	cups cooked chicken or turkey	¼	teaspoon white pepper
2	cups Cream Sauce	2	tablespoons medium sherry
¾	teaspoon salt		

Cut cooked chicken or turkey, preferably all white meat, in generous cubes (about ½ inch). In a sauté pan mix chicken or turkey with Cream Sauce, p.115, and add salt and pepper. Over low heat, heat the creamed chicken or turkey and stir in the sherry. Serve on toast points.

For variety, you may add one or more of the following:

1 cup celery, chopped and sautéed in butter
1 cup mushrooms, sliced and sautéed in butter
½ cup onion, chopped and sautéed in butter

Creamed Chicken or Turkey is wonderful for a brunch or light supper.

Our grandchildren, Jack and Lucy, in a spice stall, Istanbul, Turkey.
(Photograph taken by their mother, Elizabeth Garges Izard.)

About Sauces

At the core of Haute French Cuisine is brown stock which forms the base of many fine sauces. Most cooks, even the least experienced, have read about the day-long process of making brown stock, starting by roasting beef bones in the oven, followed by hours of simmering vegetables. Within my experience, however, even the most sophisticated home cook lacks the time or desire to create a "glossy Madeira sauce" or other sauces of that ilk.

My approach to sauces is much simpler. Many sauces are cooked in the same pan as the main dish with the leftover drippings or juices incorporated into the sauce.

Most of the light sauces are variations of basic Cream Sauce, p.115. Chicken stock is a frequent ingredient. Brown sauces generally rely on beef stock. When stock is required, I ordinarily use canned chicken or beef broth. Bouillon cubes may be substituted for either. Best of all may be the new products-Chicken Base and Beef Base that are put up in jars and kept in the refrigerator after opening.

Having expressed these generalizations, I still make simplified chicken and beef stocks when leftover bones are available. A recipe follows. Homemade stocks are more fun and probably improve flavors slightly.

Braids of garlic, Spanish village market.

Stock

Chicken, quail, beef or other bones, cooked or not

Celery ribs, in 3 to 4 inch lengths

Onions, sliced

Bay leaves

Salt

Whole black pepper corns

A chicken carcass, uncooked, boiled or baked; bones left after filleting quail; or the bones from a standing beef rib roast are suitable for making stock. Bones can also be obtained from the butcher shop. In any event, put the bones in a large saucepan or boiler and cover with water. To a typical chicken carcass, add 2 to 3 ribs of celery, a medium onion, 3 bay leaves, ¾ teaspoon salt and 10 pepper corns. Simmer over low heat, covered, for 2 to 3 hours. Replenish water as needed. At the end, let stock cook down until it is well concentrated.

Strain the stock through a colander.

Stock freezes well.

2 to 3 carrots are a good addition to beef stock.

Cream Sauce

2 tablespoons butter

2 tablespoons flour

1 cup milk

¼ teaspoon salt

⅛ teaspoon white pepper

Melt butter over low heat in a sauté pan. Gradually whisk in flour and continue whisking until mixture is smooth. Slowly whisk in milk and continue whisking until sauce is well combined and is brought to a simmer. Remove from heat and add salt and pepper.

Amount of flour may be varied from 1½ to 2½ tablespoons depending on the desired thickness of the sauce.

Makes 1 cup.

Beurre Blanc Sauce

⅓	cup white wine vinegar		Pinch of salt
⅓	cup dry white wine		Pinch of white pepper
3	tablespoons finely chopped shallots or spring onions	½	pound butter

In small saucepan boil the vinegar, white wine, shallots, salt and pepper until reduced to about 2 tablespoons. Cut butter in 12 pieces. Remove saucepan from heat and whisk in 3 pieces of butter, then add other slices one at a time whisking continuously. Put saucepan back over low heat as needed to melt butter.

For a blander sauce whisk in another stick of butter in 6 pieces.

It is apparent that Beurre Blanc is nothing but warm butter flavored with vinegar, wine, shallots, salt and pepper. The trick is to keep the butter from separating as heated butter ordinarily does. A strong acid is the catalyst that produces the desired result. Thus, it is critical that the vinegar-wine mixture be reduced to about 2 tablespoons. The sauce should be butter colored, thick and creamy – about the consistency of cream.

Chicken Barbecue Sauce

2	garlic cloves, sliced	4	dashes hot sauce
½	cup olive oil	1	teaspoon basil leaves
¼	cup lemon juice	2	tablespoons Worcestershire sauce
¼	cup red wine vinegar	½	lemon, sliced
1¼	teaspoons salt	3	tablespoons tomato paste
2	tablespoons brown sugar	3	tablespoons Madeira or sherry wine
½	teaspoon black pepper		

Cook garlic in olive oil until limp; add other ingredients and simmer for a few minutes.

Makes about 1¼ cups.

Chicken Enchiladas with Tomatillo Sauce

⅓ cup half-and-half

8 ounces softened cream cheese

3 cups cooked chicken, shredded
    (2 whole breasts)

¾ cup finely chopped onion

½ teaspoon salt

12 (8 inch) corn tortillas
    Canola or other vegetable oil

2 cups tomatillo sauce*

¾ cup grated Cheddar cheese

¾ cup grated Monterey Jack cheese

Beat together half-and-half and cream cheese. Add chicken, onion and salt. Blend well and set aside.

On a dinner plate, pour about ¼ cup canola or other vegetable oil. Lay a tortilla in the oil, then put it oil side down on a second dinner plate. Continue with tortillas until last tortilla is reached (more oil will need to be added to the plate). Dip both sides of last tortilla in oil. Microwave stack of tortillas about 30 seconds, until tortillas are soft.

Spoon a thin layer of tomatillo sauce into the bottom of 9 x 13 inch baking dish.

Place about ¼ cup chicken mixture down center of each tortilla. Roll up tortillas and place seam side down in the baking dish. Pour remaining tomatillo sauce over tortillas. Cover with foil and bake in a preheated 350 degree oven for 20 to 30 minutes-until hot. Remove foil and sprinkle enchiladas with Cheddar and Monterey Jack cheeses. Bake and/or broil the enchiladas about 5 minutes longer until cheese is melted and slightly browned.

Tomatillo sauce is available at most fine food markets.

Serves 6.

Serve enchiladas with several of the following side dishes: shredded lettuce, chopped tomatoes, sliced ripe olives, salsa and sour cream.

Charcoal Broiled Chicken

(à la Olden)

This chicken recipe launched the culinary career of my long-time hunting partner, Jack Olden. Its origins were in Birmingham, Alabama.

2   small chickens, cut in halves
(3 pound chickens are ideal)
2½   sticks butter
1   cup vinegar (white wine is good)
3   tablespoons dry mustard
(preferably Colman's)

2   tablespoons Worcestershire sauce
3   dashes hot sauce
½   teaspoon salt
¾   teaspoon freshly ground black pepper

Light charcoal and let coals reach medium heat. Set grill about 6 inches above coals. Put chicken halves on grill bone side down. Broil with the lid down. Adjust dampers to avoid flames or splash with a little water as necessary.

Let chickens broil 20 to 25 minutes before turning. Turn and broil perhaps 10 minutes on meat side, being careful not to burn.

In a small iron frying pan, melt butter and stir in vinegar. Then stir in mustard until well dissolved and add Worcestershire sauce, hot sauce, salt and pepper.

Chicken should cook about 45 minutes in all. During last 15 minutes baste frequently with the sauce on both sides. For another good barbecue sauce, see page 167.

Note that you only brush the chicken with barbecue sauce during the last 15 minutes of grilling. If you start earlier, the meat will burn and the coals are more likely to flame up. The same general rule applies to most barbecued dishes. For another good chicken barbecue sauce, see page 116.

Serves 6.

Southern Fried Chicken

2	chickens, cut up for frying (about 3 pounds each)	¾	teaspoon salt	
1	cup milk	½	teaspoon finely ground black pepper	
1	cup flour		Corn, or other vegetable oil, for frying	

Select small fryers, if available; 3 pounds or just a little less, is the perfect size. In a bowl, cover chicken pieces with milk and let soak 30 minutes to 1 hour.

In a medium bowl (or traditionally in a brown paper bag), mix flour, salt and pepper. ¾ teaspoon celery salt makes an interesting addition. Heat oil in a black cast iron skillet. The oil should be just deep enough to come up halfway on the chicken pieces (about ½ inch). Oil should be hot, but not smoking (300 to 325 degrees).

Pour milk off chicken and dredge chicken in seasoned flour, shaking off any excess flour. Place chicken pieces with bone side down in the hot oil being careful not to crowd them (oil will bubble up vigorously). Do not move chicken pieces until flour has formed a crust. In 15 to 20 minutes, chicken should be nicely browned on the bottom side. Turn chicken, cover, reduce heat slightly and continue cooking until brown on the other side (10 to 15 minutes). Heat should be adjusted so that chicken will brown within the times suggested, and the chicken will be cooked through before it becomes too brown. Turn chicken only once so as not to dislodge the crisp coating.

Remove chicken from the pan and place on absorbent paper to drain. Keep warm until ready to serve.

Serves 6 to 8.

If the South has a signature dish, fried chicken is it! The first requisite of Southern Fried Chicken is that it be cooked in a black cast iron skillet not in a deep fat fryer and certainly not in the oven. In the cast iron skillet, the cooking oil only half covers the chicken which lets the top half of the chicken steam from internal moisture while the bottom half is being fried. The chicken will have the appropriate crisp exterior, but will remain juicy and tasty on the inside.

Southern Fried Chicken is, of course, delicious served cold and is the backbone of a picnic lunch.

Fricassee Chicken

1	frying chicken, cut up for frying	½	teaspoon salt
	Vegetable oil for frying	¼	teaspoon black pepper
2	medium onions, sliced	3	egg yolks
½	cup sliced celery and celery tops	3	tablespoons cider vinegar
2	bay leaves	3	cups boiling water (approximate)

In a skillet put ¼ inch of vegetable oil. Heat oil and add chicken. Over high heat brown chicken nicely on all sides. Pour off oil and add 2 to 3 cups boiling water, onions, celery, bay leaves, salt and pepper. Cover pan and simmer until chicken is cooked through (about 45 minutes). Add hot water as needed to keep a depth of about ¾ inches. Remove chicken and onion and set aside. Let broth cool somewhat. In a small bowl, beat egg yolks and beat in vinegar and about ½ cup of the cooking broth. Then stir egg mixture into the broth and return pan to the heat. Stir until well blended and beginning to thicken (3 to 4 minutes). Put chicken and onion back in pan and heat through. Stir in more hot water if sauce gets too thick.

Serve on white rice.

Serves 4.

Fried Chicken Trinidad

1 frying chicken cut up for frying
  (about 3 pounds)
 Juice of 2 lemons
1 medium onion, sliced
4 ribs celery with tops, coarsely chopped

Salt
Black pepper
Flour
Vegetable oil for frying

Rinse chicken and put in a bowl. Sprinkle with lemon juice. Mix onion and celery with the chicken. Sprinkle chicken with salt and pepper; stir well and let stand in refrigerator for 2 to 12 hours.

Remove chicken pieces from the marinade. Season flour with salt and pepper. Toss flour with chicken pieces to coat lightly. Fill heavy iron skillet to depth of ½ inch with oil and heat. Over medium heat, cook chicken with bone side down until well browned. Turn and cook on other side until browned (30 to 40 minutes in all). Regulate heat so that chicken will cook through.

Serves 4.

Club Sandwich

A classic club sandwich consists of chicken or turkey, bacon, tomato and lettuce. It is superb. Do not add or substitute ham, cheese, smoked turkey or the like.

3 slices white bread
   Mayonnaise
3-4 thin slices cooked chicken or turkey
   (preferably white meat)
3-4 lettuce leaves

3 slices crisp bacon
½ ripe tomato, sliced
   Salt
   Black pepper

Toast regular sliced white bread and remove crusts. Spread mayonnaise on one side of 2 slices and on both sides of the third slice.

On the first slice spread the chicken or turkey slices and lettuce leaves; top with the bread slice with mayonnaise on both sides; and arrange bacon and tomato slices on top of it. Sprinkle with salt and pepper to taste and top with third slice of bread.

Secure club sandwich with 4 toothpicks and slice in half diagonally.

A supermarket near Santander, Spain.

Chicken or Turkey Hash

3	tablespoons butter		2	cups cooked chicken or turkey, cut in ½ inch dice
¼	cup finely chopped onion		1	cup boiled potatoes, peeled and cut in ¼ inch dice
2	tablespoons flour			
1½	cups chicken stock		½	teaspoon salt
¾	cup celery, cut in ¼ inch dice		¼	teaspoon black pepper

This recipe is ideal for left over chicken or turkey, but boiled fowl is as good or better.

Melt butter in a sauté pan over medium heat. Add onions and stir until onions are limp. Sprinkle in flour and continue stirring and cooking for a minute or two so that flour looses its raw taste. Continuing over medium heat, gradually whisk in stock until you have a medium thick cream sauce. Add celery and let cook for 2 to 3 minutes. Then add chicken or turkey, salt and pepper. When the poultry is well heated, add the potatoes and combine.

Serve on toast points for brunch or a light supper.

Hash freezes well.

Serves 5 to 6.

If desired you may stir in 4 tablespoons dry sherry at the end.

Chicken Piccata

1	cup flour	3-4	whole chicken breasts, halved, boned and skinned
1	teaspoon salt		
1½	teaspoons black pepper	6	ounces beer
2	teaspoons basil	¼	cup dry sherry
1	teaspoon garlic powder	¼	cup lemon juice
¼	cup olive oil		

In a small bowl, mix flour, salt, pepper, basil and garlic powder. Pour beer into another bowl. Heat oil in a large skillet over medium high heat until hot but not smoking. Dip chicken pieces in beer, shake off excess and dust with the flour mixture. Sauté chicken pieces in oil until nicely browned on both sides (about 6 minutes per side). Remove chicken. Add sherry and lemon juice to skillet and simmer about 1 minute. Return chicken to pan, cover and cook over low heat (turning once) until chicken is done (about 15 minutes). Pour sauce over chicken and serve.

Instead of chicken breasts you may use fryer pieces with the skin still on. The chicken is crisper, but the skin adds fat to the sauce.

Serves 6 to 8.

Chicken Tetrazzini

¾   pound mushrooms, thinly sliced
8   tablespoons butter (divided)
½   pound vermicelli
⅓   cup flour
3   cups chicken stock (preferably strong)
1   teaspoon salt
¼   teaspoon black pepper
⅜   teaspoon ground nutmeg

1   cup whipping cream, heated
½   cup dry sherry
4   cups cooked chicken or turkey, cut in fine strips (1½ to 2 inches long) (about 1½ pounds boned breast meat)
¼   cup grated Parmesan cheese
½   teaspoon paprika

Sauté mushrooms in 3 tablespoons butter until heated through and limp. Cook vermicelli in rapidly boiling salted water until just tender. Drain.

In a large sauté pan, melt 5 tablespoons butter and stir in flour. Gradually add stock, stirring continually, until nicely thickened. Add salt, pepper, nutmeg and hot cream and simmer, stirring often, for 5 to 10 minutes. Add sherry and stir.

Mix one-half of sauce with the vermicelli and mushrooms and put in well-buttered baking dish. Mix remaining sauce with the chicken. Make a large hole in center of the vermicelli mixture and add the chicken. Sprinkle the Tetrazzini with Parmesan cheese and paprika.

Bake in a preheated 375 degrees oven until lightly browned (about 40 minutes).

Chicken Tetrazzini freezes well. If prepared for the freezer, take it out of the oven about 10 minutes early. When ready to use, defrost and return to oven for 15 to 20 minutes until bubbling and slightly browned.

Curried Eggs

12	hard-boiled eggs, peeled	3	tablespoons white wine vinegar
¾	cup mayonnaise	½	tablespoon prepared mustard
1	teaspoon salt	1	teaspoon dry mustard
1½	tablespoons medium curry powder		Paprika and parsley for garnish
⅛	teaspoon red pepper		

Split eggs length wise. Remove yolks and blend well with the other ingredients, except paprika and parsley.

Stuff egg whites with the yolk mixture. Garnish each egg with paprika and a sprig of parsley

Charcoal Broiled Dove Breasts

18	dove breasts	3	lemons
18	thin slices bacon		Dale's steak sauce or soy sauce

Cut lemons in sixths lengthwise. Put a wedge of lemon in the cavity of each dove breast, wrap breast with a thin bacon strip and secure with a toothpick. Brush dove breasts well with Dale's sauce or soy sauce.

Let ash form on charcoal fire, but while still very hot, put dove breasts on grill about 4 inches above the coals. Cook with lid down, turning and basting with extra sauce occasionally. Remove to hot platter when bacon is nicely browned (about 10 minutes). Dove meat should be slightly pink.

Serves 5 to 6.

Mexican Dove Breasts

18 dove breasts
1 cup flour
1 tablespoon baking powder
¾ teaspoon salt
¾ teaspoon black pepper, finely ground

1 cup prepared mustard
  (French's does well)
5 tablespoons cider vinegar
8 dashes hot sauce
Vegetable oil for frying

The concept for this dove recipe comes from Frank Hines of Albany, Georgia. He discovered it in Mexico. Once again, the mustard mixture is put on last!

Mix flour and baking powder and season with salt and pepper. Mix mustard, vinegar and hot sauce. In a deep saucepan or deep sauté pan heat enough oil to cover dove breasts generously (1½ to 2 inches). Oil should be about 350 degrees.

Roll dove breasts in flour, then in the mustard mixture and drop in small batches into the hot oil (oil should sizzle up). Flour, then mustard mixture is the correct sequence! When dove breasts are nicely browned (3 to 4 minutes), remove with slotted spoon. Let dove breasts drain on absorbent paper for 4 to 5 minutes as they will continue cooking on the inside. Meat should be pink near the breast bone.

Serves 5 to 6.

Typical Argentine Asada, Estancia Quemquemtreau.

Dove Pie

(Mary Samford)

24	dove breasts	12	ounces mushrooms, thinly sliced
	Flour for dusting	3	tablespoons butter (divided)
	Salt and black pepper to taste	8	spring onions, sliced along with some of the tops
4	tablespoons bacon grease		
1	can beef gravy (8 ounce)	½	cup chopped parsley
1	can chicken broth (concentrated) (8 ounce)	1	teaspoon thyme leaves
1	can cream of mushroom soup (concentrated) (8 ounce)	¼	teaspoon hot sauce
		4	hard-boiled eggs, sliced
½	cup sherry	1	pie crust
1	cup chopped onion		

Dust dove breasts in well seasoned flour, shaking off excess flour. Heat bacon grease in cast iron skillet and brown dove breasts on all sides. Put browned dove breasts in a covered roasting pan and over them pour the beef gravy, chicken broth, mushroom soup and sherry (Do not dilute soups.) Bake, covered at 300 degrees for one hour. Remove meat from bones and return to roasting pan (leave meat in large pieces).

Sauté onion and mushrooms in 2 tablespoons butter until they take on a little color. Add sautéed onions and mushrooms, the green onions, parsley, thyme and hot sauce to the roasting pan. Simmer over direct heat for 30 more minutes. (You may do this much and hold filling in the refrigerator for a day or two or you may freeze the filling.)

When ready to make the pie, heat the filling, add the sliced hard-boiled eggs and correct the seasoning including the sherry. Place in large casserole dish, cover with pastry, brush with 1 tablespoon melted butter, cut steam vents in pastry and bake in a preheated 350 degree oven until brown and bubbly.

This recipe is a fine use for doves that have been in the freezer for a year.

At buffets this dove dish is delicious served in a chaffing dish. Omit the pastry and heat the filling before putting it in the chaffing dish.

Serves 12.

Cajun Wild Ducks

(à la Burton)

Wild ducks

Apples, cored and cut in eights

Oranges, cut in eights

Cayenne pepper

2 tablespoons vegetable oil

Flour

Pick and clean wild ducks and stuff equally with sections of apples and oranges until cavities are loosely filled. Sprinkle ducks heavily with cayenne pepper. Enough cayenne is the critical part of this recipe. Put ducks in a heavy pot with a tight lid. Pour in enough water to half cover ducks and add vegetable oil. Cover pan with a sheet of aluminum foil and then the lid.

Bake in preheated 450 degree oven for about 50 minutes for medium rare ducks which is the tender and succulent way to prepare them. Cook 10 to 15 minutes longer if you prefer to remove the pink color from the meat. Cooking time will vary depending on size and number of ducks in the pot. Suggested time is for two medium-size ducks. If ducks are large or you have more than two ducks in the pot add 10 to 15 minutes to the cooking time. In any event test for doneness by cutting a slit along the breastbone. Cook a little longer if indicated.

Discard all but about 1 ½ cups of the cooking liquid and put the pan over medium heat. As the liquid heats, whisk in enough flour to thicken it slightly. Slice ducks and pour gravy over the slices.

Celery ribs and onion sections may be substituted for the apples and oranges. The important thing is to give the insides of the ducks a clean flavor.

Gamekeeper's assistants
after a fall shoot in Wales.

Small Wild Ducks with Sausage

(Lake Charles, Louisiana)

4	small wild ducks (wood ducks or teal are fine)		Flour
1	pound bulk sausage (hot)		Salt
	Olive oil		Black pepper
		¼	cup Madeira or dry sherry

Pick, clean and rinse ducks. Cut off wings. Stuff body cavities of ducks loosely with the sausage. Cover bottom of a Dutch oven (or other heavy pot with a tight lid) with olive oil and over high heat brown ducks on all sides until virtually black. Lower heat and add enough water to half cover ducks in one layer. Simmer tightly covered over low heat for 4 to 6 hours, replenishing liquid if needed.

Remove ducks. Save about 1 cup of the pan drippings and over low heat whisk in 3 to 4 tablespoons flour. Then whisk in enough hot water to make a thick gravy. Season with salt and pepper and add about ¼ cup Madeira or dry sherry. Pour up gravy in a gravy boat.

Serve each person a whole duck with rice and gravy (a wood duck is a large serving and may be divided among light eaters). The diner should remove sausage and eat it along with the duck, rice and gravy.

The cooking time sounds long but makes a wonderfully tasty dish.

Serves 4.

Wild Duck Sauce

1	jar currant jelly (8 ounce)		Grated rind of ½ orange
½	orange, juice	1	teaspoon ground ginger
¼	lemon, juice	½	cup Madeira or Port wine

Simmer all ingredients, except wine, until well blended.

Shortly before serving stir in the Madeira or Port.

Smothered Pheasants

4	pheasants	2	medium onions, peeled and coarsely chopped (1⅔ to 2 cups)	
4	tablespoons butter	½	pound mushrooms, thickly sliced (about 2½ cups)	
4	tablespoons olive or vegetable oil			
8	tablespoons flour	1½	teaspoons salt	
1	quart half-and-half	½	teaspoon black pepper	
6	ribs celery, coarsely chopped (about 2½ cups)	¾	cup sherry	

The corn fields of South Dakota provide wonderful habitat for ring neck pheasants. River Bluff Adventures near Platte, South Dakota is the source of this pheasant recipe.

Remove leg quarters from pheasants and cut off legs at the knee joints. Remove necks and wings. With poultry shears, cut breast sections in half lengthwise. Reserve legs, wings and necks for another use.

In a large iron skillet over low heat melt butter and stir in the oil. Raise heat to medium high and lightly brown pheasant breasts and thighs on both sides. Remove pheasant pieces and put in a roasting pan. Lower the heat under the iron skillet and whisk the flour into the oil in which the pheasants were browned. Scrape up any brown bits and pieces. Increase heat slightly and gradually stir in the half-and-half. When the sauce has thickened, add the celery, onion, mushrooms, salt and pepper. Blend well. Pour sauce over the pheasant pieces. If there is not enough sauce to cover the pheasants, stir in a little milk or stock.

Bake the pheasants covered in a preheated 325 degree oven 1½ to 2 hours until the pheasants are tender. Just before removing pheasants from the oven, stir in the sherry and correct the seasoning.

Accompany this dish with wild rice. The gravy may be poured over the rice as well as the pheasants.

Serves 8.

Welsh pheasants headed to a gourmet London restaurant.

About Quail and Doves

In the Southeast, the quail has been known as the Prince of Game Birds. Following well-trained dogs, quail hunting was a popular sport throughout the twentieth century. Unfortunately, changes in land use have led to declining quail populations and decreasing availability of quail habitat.

Meanwhile, the dove population has probably increased and dove hunting is widespread. Dove shoots generally involve a number of hunters surrounding a field where the doves fly in to feed. The shoots are often accompanied by barbecues or other social events.

Quail and doves, particularly quail, are great delicacies. Traditionally, they have been smothered in a thick celery and mushroom gravy. To me, they are more flavorful in a simpler presentation, such as grilling over hot charcoal. See, Charcoal Broiled Quail, p.133, and Charcoal Broiled Dove Breasts, p.126.

Pen raised quail are now available in fine food stores.

Mallard ducks after Wales shoot.

Charcoal Broiled Quail
(John Grant's Recipe)

1   dozen quail, split down the back

Arrange quail in a wire toasting basket. Coals from an open fire pulled out on the hearth provide the ideal fuel for this dish. If this approach is not practical, use a charcoal or gas grill.

Broil quail over the coals until nicely browned. Do not overcook. Baste occasionally with the following sauce.

Sauce

¾ **pound butter**	¾ **teaspoon salt**
¾ **teaspoon freshly ground black pepper**	3 **tablespoons Worcestershire sauce**

Doves or dove breasts may be used in this recipe instead of quail. If so, spread strips of bacon over the dove breasts in the wire toasting basket.

Serves 6.

The Grants' Wildfair Plantation near Albany, Georgia was one of the finest quail hunting properties in the Southeast. After a day in the field and cocktails in the den, these quail were "The Best I Ever Tasted".

Fried Quail

8 quail, split down the back	**Black pepper**
Flour for dredging	**Vegetable oil for frying**
Salt	

Flatten quail and dredge in flour well seasoned with salt and pepper. Put about ¼ inch oil in a skillet. Fry quail over medium heat just like Southern Fried Chicken, p.119.

When well browned on all sides, remove quail and drain on absorbent paper. Do not overcook.

If you prefer quail less crisp and more tender, put the fried quail in a covered colander over boiling water and steam for 15 to 20 minutes. This last step is not followed in South Georgia, the nation's quail capital.

Serves 4.

Quail is such a delicacy that we rarely prepare it as ordinary food. People in places where quail are plentiful know better. Try Fried Quail for a treat.

Quail à la King

3	cups cooked quail, cut in strips		1	cup mushrooms, sliced
3	tablespoons butter (divided)		½	cup pimentos, cut in strips
⅓	cup flour		1	teaspoon mild curry powder
2	cups hot quail or chicken stock		1	teaspoon salt
¾	cup milk		½	teaspoon black pepper
2	egg yolks, beaten lightly		⅛	cup dry sherry

To cook quail, poach in enough water to cover. When tender, about 20 minutes, drain quail and reserve stock. Remove skin and bones and cut meat in strips.

In a small saucepan melt one tablespoon butter and whisk in flour. When well combined, whisk in stock and milk. Simmer for 5 to 7 minutes. Remove sauce from heat and beat in egg yolks.

In a sauté pan over medium heat, melt rest of butter and sauté mushrooms until limp. Add quail, mushrooms and pimentos to the sauce. Season with curry powder, salt and pepper. Heat through and stir in sherry.

Serve on buttered toast triangles.

Sautéed Quail

6	quail, split down the back	4	tablespoons Worcestershire sauce
3	tablespoons butter		Salt and pepper to taste

Flatten quail and sprinkle with salt and pepper. In a large cast iron skillet over medium heat, melt the butter. Brown quail quickly on all sides. Add about ½ cup water, cover and simmer until quail are tender (about 15 minutes). Add Worcestershire sauce and a little water and salt and pepper to taste. Blend well.

Serve on toast or rice and cover with the gravy.

Serves 4.

Quail Paprika

10	quail	1	tablespoon sweet paprika
¾	cup flour	¾	cup dry white wine
½	teaspoon salt	1	cup chicken stock
½	teaspoon black pepper	½	cup sour cream
6	tablespoons butter	2	tablespoons lemon juice
6	tablespoons finely chopped onion		

Remove breast fillets and leg quarters from quail. (Use remaining portions of quail to make quail stock). Mix flour, salt and pepper and dredge breast fillets and leg quarters lightly. Melt butter in frying pan over low heat and brown quail pieces lightly on both sides. Add chopped onion and sauté until onion starts to take on color. Sprinkle with paprika. Add wine and stock. Bring to a boil and stir up the browned bits from the bottom of the pan. Cover and simmer 5 to 10 minutes until quail are tender. If gravy is too thick, bring to desired consistency with a little water. Carefully blend in sour cream and lemon juice. Bring to simmer, but do not boil. Serve promptly.

Wild rice or white rice should accompany this dish.

You can freeze this dish before adding sour cream and lemon juice. Thaw when ready to use, heat slowly, add a little water, if needed, and carefully stir in sour cream and lemon juice. Bring to a simmer, but do not boil.

Serves 6.

Quail Paprika made exclusively from the breast fillets is an epicurean treat of the first order. The leg quarters can be cooked separately for another occasion.

Roast Stuffed Wild Turkey

1	wild turkey, picked and dressed	6-8	thin slices bacon
	Turkey or Chicken Stuffing (below) to fill cavity loosely		

Weigh oven-ready turkey before stuffing. Roast approximately 12 minutes per pound.

Prepare the stuffing. Stuff the body cavity of the turkey loosely and put a little stuffing under the skin in the breast cavity. Cover breast with bacon slices. Your turkey is now ready for the oven.

Put turkey on a rack in a shallow roasting pan. Roast in a preheated 350 degree oven for the time indicated. About 20 minutes before the turkey is done, remove the bacon slices so that the breast will brown nicely. Test turkey for doneness; a slit next to the breast bone should reveal pinkish meat, but should not be red at center. If red, roast for another 12 minutes. Do not over cook, or the meat will not be moist.

Let turkey sit 10 minutes or so before carving. Remember that the meat continues to cook during this period.

A 12 to 15 pound turkey serves 12 comfortably.

Turkey or Chicken Stuffing

2	sticks butter	¼	cup chopped parsley
1¼	cups chopped onion	½	teaspoon ground sage
1¼	cups chopped celery	½	teaspoon thyme
24	slices stale white bread, crusts removed and cut in 1 inch cubes*	2	teaspoons salt
		1	teaspoon black pepper

Melt the butter in a cast iron skillet. Add the onion and celery and sauté until they take on a little color.

Put the bread cubes in a large bowl and stir in the onion, celery, butter mixture and parsley. Mix well. Add the sage, thyme, salt and pepper and mix. Loosely stuff your bird.

*If the bread is too fresh, bake the cubes in a slow oven for a few minutes.

Makes enough stuffing for a 12 to 15 pound turkey.

Citrus Marinated Turkey Breast

(Charcoal Broiled)

1	turkey breast (6 to 7 pounds)	3	tablespoons cider vinegar
1¼	cups orange juice	2	teaspoons salt
¼	cup lime juice	1	teaspoon black pepper
¼	cup olive oil	2	teaspoons oregano leaves

Remove and discard skin and breast bone from turkey. Place breast halves in a jumbo, heavy duty, zip-top plastic bag; set aside (most meat departments will gladly bone turkey breasts).

Combine remaining ingredients to form a marinade. Mix well. Set ¾ cup marinade aside. Pour remainder of marinade over turkey in the zip-top bag and seal bag. Chill 8 hours, turning bag occasionally.

Remove turkey from marinade. Cook turkey, with the grill lid closed, over hot coals about 18 minutes on each side, brushing occasionally with the reserved marinade. Let stand 10 minutes before slicing. Warm the reserved marinade and serve with the sliced turkey.

Serves 6 to 8.

To cook turkey in the oven, place on a rack in a roasting pan; bake in preheated 325 degree oven for 1 hour and 10 minutes brushing with marinade as above.

The author with a fine wild turkey.

Meat

Gauchos herding beef cattle near the Malleo River, a premier Argentine trout stream.

Meat

Overcooking is by far the most common cause of unappetizing meat dishes. Heat removes the juices and makes meat stringy and tough. Rare to medium rare has been generally recognized as the preferred way to serve beef. Lamb has joined the ranks and is now served pink or rarer. The other white meat, pork, probably remains an exception, although the best chefs cook it barely beyond the pink stage.

For many years, we visited a West Yellowstone guest ranch which prided itself on its gourmet cuisine. One of the weekly highlights was a standing prime rib roast which was always cooked on the rare side. Occasionally guests complained and requested their meat "well done". The owner who presided at the carving station ceremoniously returned a couple of slices of beef to the kitchen where they were turned brown by dipping in warm beef consommé. The owner reported that these guests frequently complimented "the best roast beef they had ever tasted."

Stews and chilis are exceptions to these considerations. Long boiling or braising reverses the process and tenderizes meat. Also in such dishes the flavor of the meat is secondary with the focus on vegetables and seasoning.

Fine aged hams, Municipal Market, Irun, Spain.

Corned Beef Hash

2	cups cooked corned beef	½	cup onion (about 1 medium onion)
2	cups boiled potatoes	⅓	teaspoon freshly ground black pepper
	(about 2 large baking potatoes)	4	tablespoons butter (divided)
½	cup green bell pepper	½	cup milk
	(about ½ bell pepper)		

Cut corned beef in chunks and pulse in food processor fitted with the steel blade until corned beef is about the consistency of hamburger. An easier alternative is to grind the corned beef in a meat grinder fitted with the coarse blade. It helps to leave some fat on the beef. Boil potatoes in their jackets until thoroughly cooked and quite soft. Cool, then peel and cut in ¼ inch dice. Finely chop green pepper and onion.

Melt 3 tablespoons butter in a skillet over medium heat and add green pepper and onion. Stir until limp (about 3 minutes). Add and thoroughly mix corned beef, potatoes and pepper. Stir in milk. Taste for salt; generally corned beef provides enough salt by itself. At this point you may hold hash in the refrigerator for a couple of days or freeze it for later use.

In a buttered skillet form a layer of hash ½ to ¾ inch thick. Press hash down and cook over medium heat until a crust forms on bottom. Invert pan and turn hash out on a platter. Poached eggs are traditionally served on top of corned beef hash. Tomato catsup (preferably warmed) is a welcome condiment.

Serves 6 to 8.

Instead of cooking in a cake, you may form hash into patties, dust with flour and sauté in butter over medium high heat until nicely browned on both sides.

Enormous ranches in the Patagonia section of Argentina raise beef for the local table as well as for export. Argentine beef is typically grass fed and is not fattened in stock yards. The meat is, therefore, leaner and more flavorful, but tends to be tough by American standards.

Curry Side Dishes

Curries are greatly enhanced by a variety of side dishes. Long grain rice should be passed first followed by the curry and then the side dishes in individual bowls.

I recommend most of the following with every curry:

Onions, finely chopped	**Mango chutney, chopped** (Major Grey's is excellent)
Crisp bacon, crumbled	
Hard-boiled eggs, chopped	**Chopped nuts, usually peanuts or almonds**

After the above suggestions your imagination is the limit. Often used (all peeled and chopped) are:

Apples	**Melons**
Cucumbers	**Pickles**
Grapes	**Ripe olives**
Grated coconut	**Tomatoes**
Green peppers	

For a large dinner party, a curry is ideal served buffet style. Start with large bowls for the rice and curry. After that smaller bowls for the side dishes should be arranged on the buffet table. Each guest then decides which side dishes to add to his curry and rice.

Beef Jerky

(Martha Wayt)

Flank steak or brisket	**Lemon pepper seasoning** (Lawry's is excellent)
Soy sauce	**Garlic salt**

Remove all fat from meat. Cut steak with the grain in foot-long strips, ⅛ to ¼ inches thick, ¼ to ⅜ inches wide. Generously coat strips of meat with soy sauce and let stand 1 to 3 hours. Lay meat strips on waxed paper and sprinkle liberally with lemon pepper and lightly with garlic salt, turning once to be sure both sides are coated.

Place meat strips carefully on a broiler rack. Put pans underneath the racks to catch drippings. Bake meat strips at 150 degrees for 12 hours or until meat is dried and tacky.

Jerky keeps indefinitely in the refrigerator.

Curried Beef Stew

4	slices bacon
4	tablespoons butter (divided)
2	medium yellow onions, cut in medium slices
¾	cup flour
1	teaspoon salt
½	teaspoon black pepper
2½	tablespoons medium curry powder

3	pounds top round or sirloin of beef, cut in 1 inch cubes
4	bay leaves
2	cups celery, diced (¼ inch)
1½	cups carrots, scraped and sliced (¼ inch)
3	cups new potatoes, peeled and diced (¼ inch)
1½	cups frozen baby lima beans
3	tablespoons lemon juice

In a Dutch oven or heavy pan, cook bacon (cut in 1 inch lengths), 2 tablespoons butter and onions together until onions are golden brown. Remove onions and bacon and reserve. Season flour with salt, pepper and curry powder and dredge meat in it. Add remaining butter to pan and brown meat on all sides. Sprinkle excess flour over meat. Add bay leaves, reserved onion and bacon and enough water to cover the meat. Simmer covered for about 45 minutes (adding more water if needed). Stir occasionally.

Add celery, carrots and potatoes and simmer covered about 45 minutes longer. Add lima beans and lemon juice; correct seasoning and simmer 15 to 20 minutes longer (uncovered if gravy seems a little thin).

Remove bay leaves and thicken gravy with a little flour, if needed.

One half of this recipe works well.

Serves 8 to 10.

Curry from Leftovers

(Lamb, Chicken, Shrimp)

Curry powder is unpredictable and quantities are necessarily approximate. If you have strong curry powder, use less than the quantity specified. Taste! You can always add more curry powder.

2	tablespoons butter	1½-2	tablespoons medium curry powder
1	medium onion, chopped	2	tablespoons flour
½	green bell pepper, chopped	¼	teaspoon ground ginger
2	ribs celery, chopped	1	teaspoon salt
3-4	cups cooked shrimp, chicken, lamb or other meat, cut in ½ inch cubes	⅛	teaspoon red pepper
2	cups stock, chicken for seafood, beef for meat (divided)	2	tablespoons lemon juice
		½	cup cream

In large sauté pan melt butter; add onion, bell pepper and celery; and simmer until limp. Then add meat with 1 cup stock. Bring to a simmer. Mix curry powder, flour, ginger, salt and red pepper. Stir into sauté pan and add the other cup of stock. Cook until well blended, adding more liquid (stock or water) if needed. Just before serving, stir in lemon juice and cream. Adjust the seasoning and serve with white rice.

One half cup of applesauce is a pleasant addition for a slightly sweeter curry. Just stir in after the flour. The usual Curry Side Dishes are recommended, p.142.

Chili Con Carne

(Ground Beef)

½ pound pinto beans	2½ tablespoons chili powder
1½ pounds ground beef	3 teaspoons salt
1 large onion, thinly sliced	½ teaspoon black pepper
½ cup bacon grease	⅛ teaspoon red pepper
4 garlic cloves, minced	3 cups condensed tomato soup
2½ tablespoons ground cumin (comino)	2 cups water

Soak pinto beans in cold water overnight. Drain beans, put in saucepan and cover with fresh water. Simmer until beans are almost tender (about 1 hour). Drain.

In a skillet, brown garlic and onion in bacon grease; then brown the ground beef in batches. In a large saucepan, mix beans, garlic, onion, beef, and all other ingredients and simmer at least 1 hour, preferably longer.

Venison hamburger is an excellent substitute for beef.

Chili Con Carne Y Frijoles

(Stew Meat)

My aunt Margaret always bragged about the wonderful chili that she had in Texas early in the twentieth century. She particularly recalled that the chili was made from stew meat, rather than the hamburger that is so prevalent today. This was our effort to reconstruct her Texas recipe.

1	pound pinto beans or red kidney beans or a combination of both
5	tablespoons bacon grease
4	medium onions, sliced
3	cloves garlic, sliced
3	pounds beef chuck cut in ½ inch cubes (remove as much fat as possible) (weigh after trimming)
7	cups canned tomatoes and juice (2 - 28 ounce cans) (peeled, diced tomatoes do well)
2-3	tablespoons chili powder (depending on taste and strength of chili powder)
2½	teaspoons ground cumin (comino)
½	teaspoon oregano leaves, crushed
½	teaspoon red pepper flakes
1	tablespoon salt

Soak beans overnight. Then cover beans with water and simmer until almost tender (about 1 hour). Melt grease in a large skillet and sauté onions and garlic until they are limp and take on a little color. Remove onions and garlic and brown meat on all sides. Return onions and garlic to pan with meat and add rest of ingredients except beans; simmer about 2½ hours with top off; stir occasionally. If you are making large quantities, a wok works very well to sauté onions and garlic and brown meat.

Then add beans to chili and simmer until meat and beans are tender (1 to 1½ hours).

Chili reheats and freezes well.

Makes about 3½ quarts.

Venison instead of beef is very good in this recipe.

This chili is delicious served with large fritos, guacamole salad and plenty of cold beer.

Butcher shop, Oxford, England.

Butcher, Municipal Market, Oxford, England.

Empanadas de Carne

2	medium onions, finely chopped	1	teaspoon oregano
1	bunch green scallions	1	teaspoon salt
4	beef bouillon cubes	3	tablespoons sugar
4	tablespoons paprika	½	cup chopped green olives
1	teaspoon black pepper	½-1	cup raisins
½	cup butter	3	eggs, hard-boiled and chopped
2½-3	pounds chopped sirloin	2	egg yolks, beaten

Dough for Tapas

3½	cups self-rising flour	⅓	cup vegetable oil
1	cup water		

Put about 1 inch of water in a large skillet and add onions, scallions, bouillon cubes, paprika, pepper and butter. Bring to a boil and stir for 3 to 5 minutes. Add chopped sirloin, mix and cook slightly (do not cook through). Add oregano, salt and sugar and continue stirring mixture. Do not overcook, as meat will finish cooking in the oven. Remove mixture from heat. Stir in olives, raisins and hard-boiled eggs. Leave in refrigerator overnight for the mixture to congeal.

Use empanada tapas (available at some fine food stores) or make dough by combining ingredients specified above. If making own dough, roll it about ⅛ inch thick on a floured surface and cut into rounds about 4 inches in diameter. Place 1 to 2 tablespoons of the cold meat mixture in the center of each tapa, moisten the edges with a little water, fold over and pinch edges to close. Brush the tops of the prepared empanadas with egg yolk to give them a golden color.

Grease a cookie sheet with butter or cooking spray, arrange empanadas in a single layer, and cook in a preheated 350 degree oven for approximately 20 minutes until nicely browned.

Argentine cook making empanadas.

Flank Steak or London Broil
(Charcoal Broiled)

2   pounds flank steak

Marinade

2   tablespoons olive oil

2   tablespoons lemon juice

2   garlic cloves, sliced

½   teaspoon salt

½   teaspoon freshly ground black pepper

1   tablespoon parsley, chopped

2   tablespoons butter

Mix marinade and heat sufficiently to melt butter. Pour marinade into a flat dish and marinate steak for ½ to 1 hour. Turn 2 or 3 times.

Sauce

1   pound mushrooms, sliced

4   tablespoons butter (divided)

1   clove garlic, sliced

2   tablespoons flour

½   cup beef broth

½   cup water

½   teaspoon salt

½   teaspoon black pepper

1½   tablespoons lemon juice

1½   tablespoons Worcestershire sauce

2   tablespoons fresh basil, thyme or similar fresh herb, shredded

In a sauté pan over medium heat, cook mushrooms in 2 tablespoons butter until slightly browned. Set pan aside.

Meanwhile, in a small saucepan, melt 2 tablespoons butter over low heat; simmer garlic until soft; and then gradually work in flour. When well blended slowly add beef broth and water stirring until brought to a boil. Add remaining ingredients and blend well. If sauce gets too thick, stir in a little more water.

Remove steak from marinade and broil over a hot charcoal fire about 5 minutes on one side. Turn, baste with remaining marinade and broil about 5 minutes more. Steak should be medium rare.

Reheat sauté pan with mushrooms and pour sauce into it. Heat through. As flank steak tends to be a little tough, cut it in thin slices across the grain. Pour sauce over steak and serve.

Serves 4 to 6.

About Hamburgers

According to culinary lore, seamen from the port of Hamburg, Germany brought the word, hamburger, to the United States. At any rate it first appeared in print about 1890 and the modern version in a bun was introduced at the St. Louis World Fair of 1904.

In the 1930's, hamburgers were featured in every little diner of which there were a great many prior to McDonalds and other chains. Short-order cooks presided over their greasy griddles and passed the time mashing hamburgers with their large metal spatulas. As far as I know, James Beard, in one of his early publications, was the first to point out that mashing a hamburger removed all its juices and made it dry and tough.

Like most beef dishes, a hamburger should be cooked rare to medium rare. Not too long ago concern over food-borne bacteria led to a ban on rare hamburgers, but that ban has largely dissipated. Through it all, Beef Tartare, p.158, continued unchallenged.

Hamburgers may be made from ground sirloin, round steak or chuck or just ground beef. The fat content varies from normal to less than 5 percent. To my mind the best hamburgers are made from sirloin with normal fat content. Certainly extra lean meat leads to a dry hamburger.

Besides being medium rare, a good hamburger should be well browned on both sides. This is no easy feat. To begin with, the burger should be at least 1 inch thick. An iron skillet should be heated extremely hot wiped with oil and the burger quickly seared on both sides. At this point the burger will probably have reached medium rare. Remember that meat continues cooking after being removed from the heat. If cooking over charcoal, make the burgers a little thicker and have the fire extremely hot and close to the meat.

For condiments, I like a thin slice of onion, a generous sprinkle of freshly ground black pepper and tomato ketchup. Others can have their mustard, mayonnaise, pickles, lettuce and sliced tomatoes. Chopped onions and other seasoning may be added to the hamburger meat (Savory Hamburgers, p.152).

The best commercial hamburgers I ever tasted were at the Hamburger Heaven chain in New York in the 1950's. Those hamburgers were cooked in a gas broiler. I was told by one of their managers that the secret to their special flavor was the use of unaged beef. At the opposite end of the spectrum, and contradicting all of my advice, the thin, little hamburgers at the Krystal chain served with chopped onion, mustard and a pickle slice have an unforgettable flavor, particularly if accented with black pepper. In the old days these hamburgers were 10 cents each.

Savory Hamburgers

1½ pounds ground beef (chuck or sirloin)
4 tablespoons finely chopped onion
3 tablespoons Worcestershire sauce

1 teaspoon coarse ground black pepper
Vegetable oil

In a bowl combine foregoing ingredients. Shape into bun-size patties about an inch thick. Heat a heavy iron skillet until very hot and rub with oil. Sear hamburgers until crusty brown on one side. Turn and sear the other side. Hamburgers should be rare at this point. If you prefer meat medium, cover pan, reduce heat and let cook for another minute or so. See About Hamburgers, p.151, for Charcoal Broiling.

Serve hamburgers on toasted buns with thin sliced onions, tomato ketchup and freshly ground black pepper. Some people prefer prepared mustard in addition to or instead of ketchup.

The same hamburger mixture can be shaped into larger hamburger steaks. After browning steaks on one side, cook with the top on so that meat will not be too rare in the center. Being thicker, hamburger steaks are easier to cook over charcoal.

Serves 6 (only 4 if you make hamburger steaks).

Tuscan Meatloaf
(Hot or Cold)

½	cup chopped onion	½	teaspoon basil
1	large clove garlic, minced	½	teaspoon oregano
3	tablespoons butter	¼	teaspoon fennel seed
1	egg	¼	cup chopped parsley
½	cup milk	1	teaspoon salt
2	slices white bread (crusts removed)	½	teaspoon freshly ground black pepper
½	teaspoon sweet paprika	1	pound ground round steak

Sauté onion and garlic in butter until just limp.

In large mixing bowl, beat egg lightly. Stir in milk. Tear each slice of bread in small pieces (the size of a dime or smaller) and add to milk along with paprika, basil, oregano, fennel seed, parsley, salt and pepper. Mix well. Add onion-garlic-butter and mix. Then add meat to the milk mixture. With hands, quickly incorporate meat. Do not overwork. Shape meat mixture into a loaf and place in a loaf baking pan. Do not fill pan too full as juices will boil over.

Bake meatloaf in preheated 350 degree oven for 1 hour. Pour off excess pan drippings and let stand 10 to 15 minutes.

To make gravy, put 4 to 5 tablespoons drippings from the pan in a sauté pan. Over medium heat, stir in 3 to 4 tablespoons flour. Lightly brown flour and then stir in enough milk or water to make a smooth gravy. Season with salt and black pepper.

Like many meatloafs, this meatloaf may be best served cold. After cooling, wrap and store in the refrigerator. Serve on crusty bread with lots of mustard and a cold beer.

Roast Prime Ribs of Beef

If possible obtain the smallest end of the prime ribs. The smaller slices make nicer servings, and the small end contains relatively less fat. Leaving the bones in the standing roast adds to the flavor and makes a more handsome presentation. It is no more difficult to carve.

	Standing prime rib roast	½	teaspoon thyme
	Vegetable oil	½	teaspoon turmeric
4	medium cloves garlic, minced	1½	teaspoons coarse ground black pepper
1	tablespoon salt		

Rub roast with vegetable oil. In a mortar with a pestle, mash garlic and salt together. Stir in thyme, turmeric and pepper. Rub the garlic-spice mixture into the meat and fat sides of the roast.

Put roast, rib side down, on a rack in an uncovered roasting pan in a preheated 450 degree oven. After 30 minutes, reduce heat to 325 degrees and continue roasting for the total time indicated below (times are for medium rare which is the only way to serve prime ribs).

Time varies with the number of ribs.

2	rib roast, 20 minutes per pound
3	rib roast, 19 minutes per pound
4	rib or larger roast, 17 to 18 minutes per pound

Remove roast from oven and let rest 10 to 15 minutes before carving.

If you prefer, you may omit the oil, garlic and spices. Just rub the roast with a generous amount of salt and freshly ground black pepper.

Chimichurri Sauce

(From an Argentine Housewife)

4	cloves garlic, chopped	1	teaspoon basil
1	pickled banana pepper, minced (scant teaspoon)	1	teaspoon oregano
		½	teaspoon crushed red pepper flakes
1	teaspoon salt	½	teaspoon rosemary
4	tablespoons vinegar	2	pinches black pepper
2	teaspoons minced parsley	1	cup olive oil

Put garlic, pickled pepper and salt in a mortar (or food processor) and crush until they become a thick paste. Add the vinegar and the rest of the ingredients, except the olive oil. Mix well. Let the mixture stand for 3 to 4 hours and then stir in the olive oil. Age for 3 to 4 days before using.

Chimichurri Sauce keeps several weeks in the refrigerator.

Makes about 1 cup.

Argentines keep this sauce in their pantries and use it regularly on beef and other meats cooked at their frequent asadas.

Crème Fraîche

1	cup whipping cream	1-1½ tablespoons buttermilk or 3 tablespoons sour cream

In jar, combine ingredients. Cover jar tightly and shake for at least 1 minute. Let jar stand at room temperature for at least 8 hours, or until the cream is thick (may take as long as 24 hours).

Store Crème Fraîche in refrigerator. Keeps 2 to 4 weeks.

Makes about 1 cup.

Crème Fraîche is a mainstay of French cooking. It is more delicate than sour cream, but imparts a tart taste not present in ordinary cream. It is most frequently used as a principal ingredient for sauces or soups because it can be boiled without curdling. It may also be spooned over fresh fruits or warm cobblers.

Steak au Poivre

This recipe for the first steak au poivre that I encountered came from a wonderful little restaurant in Paris during the mid 1950's. The crème was called crème reversé and was almost solid. It came in a gallon tin. Crème fraîche is the closest available substitute, but sour cream may be used. The chef actually covered the steaks with a solid layer of whole black peppercorns. Many were dislodged before eating, and the dish did not seem too hot. Somehow with modern pepper, it may be better to settle for a scattered layer of peppercorns in today's rendition of this famous recipe.

3	pounds beef steak (either strip sirloin, delmonico steaks or filet mignon cut about 1½ inches thick)		Salt to taste
		3-4	tablespoons brandy
		6-8	tablespoons Crème Fraîche
	Whole black peppercorns to taste	2	tablespoons butter

Cover steaks on both sides with a solid layer of whole black peppercorns and press peppercorns into meat. Salt liberally. Melt a little steak fat in a hot cast iron frying pan. Add steaks and sear on both sides. Reduce heat and cook to desired doneness, turning once or twice. Pour brandy into pan and ignite. Lower heat. Stir in Crème Fraîche, p.155, and the butter. Pour sauce over steaks.

Serves 4.

Hash

2	cups leftover cooked meat (lamb, beef, chicken, duck), coarsely chopped	2	tablespoons flour
1	cup chopped onion	½	teaspoon salt
1	cup chopped celery	⅛	teaspoon black pepper
1	cup sliced mushrooms	1	cup chicken or beef stock
3	tablespoons butter		Chopped parsley for garnish

Over medium heat, melt butter in a sauté pan and sauté onions, celery and mushrooms for about 5 to 8 minutes. Add meat and mix with the vegetables; sprinkle with flour; and stir well. Add broth while stirring. Continue cooking, stirring occasionally, until hash is smooth and thickened. Sprinkle with parsley.

Serves 4 to 5.

Fillet of Beef Stroganoff

2   tablespoons oil

2   tablespoons butter

1½   pounds fillet of beef, cut in 1 inch slices

     Salt and freshly ground black pepper to taste

3   tablespoons finely chopped shallots

⅓   teaspoon hot sauce

½   teaspoon crumbled tarragon

1   tablespoon Worcestershire sauce

1-1½   cups sour cream

     Parsley for garnish

This quickly prepared stroganoff, using top quality meat, is tender and flavorful. It is true to original stroganoff recipes. Today's more common braised meat stroganoff does not do justice to the original concept.

In an iron skillet over high heat melt butter and oil. When bubbly, quickly cook fillet slices until browned on both sides, but still quite pink inside (about 2 minutes per side). Salt and pepper to taste and remove fillets to a hot platter.

Add the shallots and more salt and pepper to the skillet. When shallots are wilted, add and combine the hot sauce, tarragon and Worcestershire sauce. Blend thoroughly.

Remove the skillet from the heat and carefully stir in the sour cream. Just heat through. Boiling will cause the sauce to curdle. Spoon sauce over the fillets and garnish with parsley.

Rounds of fried toast topped with sautéed mushrooms are an excellent accompaniment.

A slow afternoon. Street market, Luxor, Egypt.

Beef Tartare

My first recollection of Beef Tartare was at the old Men's Grill in the Mayflower Hotel, Washington, D.C. The various ingredients were brought to the table in small dishes and ceremoniously mixed by the maitre d'.

¼ pound very lean round steak, ground twice

1 tablespoon finely chopped onion

1 tablespoon capers

½ teaspoon prepared mustard (preferably English or other hot mustard)

1½ tablespoons Worcestershire sauce

Freshly ground black pepper (generous amount)

¼ teaspoon salt

1 egg yolk

Mix ground steak, onion, capers, mustard, Worcestershire sauce, pepper and salt until well distributed. Add egg yolk and mix (egg yolk may be omitted, if you have an aversion to raw eggs).

Serve Beef Tartare on lettuce leaves as an appetizer; or as an hors d'oeuvre, mound tartare in the center of a serving plate and surround with thin slices of party rye, white toast or saltines.

Deviled Calf's Liver

4 slices tender calf's liver (about ½ inch thick and well trimmed)

Flour for dusting

Salt and black pepper to taste

2 tablespoons butter

2 cloves garlic, chopped

1½ teaspoons dry mustard

1 tablespoon Worcestershire sauce

1 tablespoon tarragon vinegar (or lemon juice)

2 tablespoons water

Parsley and/or fresh tarragon, chopped

Use only young, tender liver that is very light in color. Do not overcook. Dredge liver in flour seasoned with salt and pepper. Melt butter in a skillet until bubbly and sauté liver very rapidly until pale pink in the center (about 2 minutes per side). Remove liver.

Add remaining ingredients and more butter if needed to the skillet. Stir with pan juices until blended. Pour sauce over liver. Sprinkle with parsley and/or tarragon. Serve immediately.

Serves 4.

Lamb Curry

3	pounds boneless shoulder or leg of lamb, cut in 1 inch cubes	½	lemon, thinly sliced
4	tablespoons butter or olive oil	4	medium apples, peeled, cored and coarsely chopped
4	medium onions, coarsely chopped	1½	cups chicken broth
6	garlic cloves, finely chopped	1½	teaspoons salt
1½-2	tablespoons medium curry powder	⅓	teaspoon coarsely ground black pepper

In a sauté pan, brown the lamb in the butter or olive oil. Remove lamb and set aside. Add the onions and garlic to the oil remaining in the pan and sauté, stirring constantly, until onions are soft, but not brown. Add curry powder and cook, still stirring, for 2 to 4 minutes. Put meat back in pan. Stir in lemon slices, apples, chicken broth, salt and pepper. Bring to boil; cover and simmer 1½ to 2 hours. Stir occasionally. If too runny, simmer with lid off. After an hour or so, correct the seasoning.

Serves 6.

Serve with rice and the usual Curry Side Dishes, p.142.

Roasting lambs on a rainy Easter morning in Greece.

Celebrating Easter in Greece begins at midnight Saturday following evening church services. On Sunday morning, each village has its communal barbecue of whole lambs accompanied by generous amounts of local wine with its distinctive resin flavor. Every passerby is welcomed and offered samples of lamb and wine.

Trinidad Lamb Curry

(Phyllis)

5 pounds lamb, cut in 1 inch cubes

1 medium onion, coarsely chopped

2 tablespoons chopped celery leaves (packed)

1 tablespoon lemon juice

1 tablespoon cider vinegar

2 tablespoons soy sauce

1½ teaspoons angostura bitters

2 teaspoons salt

1 teaspoon black pepper

1 teaspoon paprika

Wash meat and drain. Put meat in a bowl and add all other ingredients; mix everything together. Let stand for about 2 hours or overnight

To Prepare Curry

2 tablespoons sugar

2½ tablespoons vegetable oil

2 tablespoons medium curry powder

Put sugar and vegetable oil in sauté pan over medium high heat and simmer until sugar becomes dark brown. Add meat which has been removed from the marinade and brown. Sprinkle the curry powder over the meat. Add marinade, cover and simmer over low heat until meat is tender (about 1½ hours). Stir occasionally and add more water, if needed. If sauce has not begun to thicken, cook uncovered for last half hour or so.

Serve with rice and a selection of Curry Side Dishes, p.142.

Lamb in Dill Sauce

(Sweden)

4 pounds breast or shoulder of lamb, cut in 1 inch cubes

4-5 cups water

Bouquet of 1 bay leaf, 5 sprigs fresh dill and 5 sprigs parsley, tied together with a string

1 teaspoon salt

1 teaspoon whole peppercorns, white if available

Remove bone and excess fat from lamb. In a heavy 4 to 6 quart casserole, cover lamb with water and bring to boil over high heat. Lower heat to moderate and skim off scum as it rises to the surface. Add the bouquet and salt and peppercorns. Partially cover pot and simmer very slowly for about 1½ hours. Remove lamb to a deep platter or casserole dish, cover and keep warm in a 200 degree oven. Strain lamb stock through a fine sieve and boil down rapidly until reduced to 2 cups.

Dill Sauce

2 tablespoons butter

2 tablespoons flour

2 cups reduced lamb stock (from above)

5 tablespoons fresh dill, chopped in ½ inch lengths and firmly packed

1 tablespoon white wine vinegar

2 teaspoons sugar

¼ teaspoon black pepper

1 teaspoon lemon juice

1 egg yolk, lightly beaten

Dill sprigs for garnish

Lemon slices for garnish

Melt 2 tablespoons butter in a saucepan. Remove from heat and whisk in 2 tablespoons flour. Return to low heat and add stock stirring rapidly with a whisk. Bring sauce to a boil, whisking constantly, until thick. Simmer 5 minutes stirring frequently. Add dill, vinegar, sugar, pepper and lemon juice. Stir 2 tablespoons of the hot sauce into egg yolk then pour yoke mixture into sauce continuing to stir. Heat again and correct seasoning. Pour over lamb. Garnish with dill sprigs and lemon slices.

Good with boiled new potatoes or rice.

Lamb with Green Beans

1½ pounds fresh green beans, cut in 2 inch lengths

4 tablespoons olive oil

2 pounds boneless stewing lamb, in 1 inch cubes

2 cups chopped onion

4 cups medium ripe tomatoes, peeled, seeded and coarsely chopped (6 to 8 medium tomatoes)

1¼ teaspoons salt

1 teaspoon freshly ground black pepper

¾ teaspoon freshly ground nutmeg

¾ teaspoon ground allspice

Spread beans in the bottom of 4 to 6 quart casserole dish.

In a cast iron frying pan, heat oil over moderate heat. Add lamb and brown nicely. As the lamb browns, transfer it to the casserole on top of the beans. Cook onions in oil until they take on a little color (about 5 minutes). Spread onions over lamb and beans and then add tomatoes. Sprinkle with salt, pepper, nutmeg and allspice. Place casserole over low heat, cover tightly, and simmer without stirring-about 1 hour or until beans are tender. Serve at once, preferably with rice.

One-half recipe works well in a 2 quart casserole dish.

Serves 8.

Roast Leg of Lamb

(Mallory's Recipe)

6-7 pound leg of spring lamb
    Cider vinegar
    Bacon grease

    Salt
    Freshly ground black pepper
    Flour

Contrary to the old-fashioned view, lamb is much more flavorful when not overcooked. Slightly pink in the center is ideal although many people prefer lamb even rarer.

Leave skin on leg of lamb. Wash well, rub with cider vinegar and bacon grease and then sprinkle heavily with salt, freshly ground black pepper and a little flour.

Place on a rack in a 325 degree preheated oven. From time to time brush lamb with:

Sauce

2   tablespoons Worcestershire sauce
2   dashes hot sauce
2   tablespoons olive oil
2   cloves garlic, minced

Cook 20 minutes per pound for meat that will still be pink in the center; 30 minutes per pound for medium (slightly less time per pound if leg is over 7 pounds).

Lamb cooking in front of open fire, Estancia Arroyo Verde, Argentina.

About Charcoal Broiling

The apocryphal discovery of grilled meat is traced by Charles Lamb, in his delightful nineteenth century essay, A Dissertation on Roast Pig. He describes how a pig was caught in a burning house in a small village in China. The natives' joyful reaction to the first taste of charred meat foreshadowed the development of barbecue cults all over the world.

Reflections of this common ancestry are widespread. To mention a few: Argentina has its asadas with whole lambs impaled on sword-like frames before an open fire (see picture p.163) to be served with Chimichurri Sauce, p.155; Greece also barbecues whole lambs but turns them on spits over hot coals (see picture p.159); Yugoslavia cooks chunks of meat on an open hearth in Alpine resorts; and, of course, we in the South cook whole hogs over coals shoveled into pits dug in the ground (see picture p.169).

Incidentally the use of whole animals is faithful to the derivation of the word barbecue; from the French: "barbe à queue" - from whiskers to tail.

After the open hearth, charcoal grills developed and meat was cooked in more manageable cuts. Also use of the grill spread to seafood and now to vegetables as well. Today sophisticated gas fired grills are making old fashioned charcoal obsolete. They do a good job on a broad range of ingredients. Traditional charcoal is, however, still my favorite. It can produce a very hot fire to sear food from steak to salmon and imparts a distinctive flavor.

Attesting to the taste of the real thing, Baccanalia, one of Atlanta's premier new restaurants, grills its beef, lamb, pork and poultry over a flaming oak fire in its shining, stainless-steel kitchen.

Charcoal broiled recipes in this book will work on either charcoal or gas grills. They may also be cooked under a conventional broiler or other indoor grill.

Charcoal broiled recipes are collected under the heading, "Charcoal Broiled", in the Index.

Smoking is another off shoot of the barbecue grill. The range of this cookbook does not cover that field, but does include a recipe for Smoked Whitefish, p.28.

Charcoal Broiled Leg of Lamb

1   leg of lamb (4 to 7 pounds)

Have butcher butterfly the leg of lamb. Remove skin, gristle and excess fat. Spread lamb out flat on a cookie pan or in a roasting pan.

Sprinkle lamb on both sides with the following ingredients in the order listed:

Juice of 3 lemons

6   tablespoons olive oil

3   tablespoons Worcestershire sauce

2   tablespoons lemon pepper seasoning (Lawry's is excellent)

2   teaspoons freshly ground black pepper

Let lamb marinate 4 to 8 hours. Turn once or twice.

If you have a long-handled toasting basket, it will help keep the lamb compact, but you can put the lamb directly on the charcoal grill. Cook lamb over medium hot charcoal for about 15 minutes per side. Thicker part of meat should be nice and pink inside. Thinner parts will be medium to well done. Baste occasionally with remainder of marinade.

Slice lamb across the grain as you would a steak. This lamb is also good cold.

Four pound legs of spring lamb are hard to find these days but do beautifully in this recipe and will serve 5 or 6 people. Five to 6 pound legs are fine and serve 8 or so. Seven pound legs start getting a little thick but may be used.

Lamb Shish Kebabs

¼ cup olive oil
¼ cup lemon juice
3 tablespoons red wine vinegar
1 medium onion, thinly sliced
1 teaspoon coriander
1 teaspoon powered ginger
1 garlic clove, mashed
2 teaspoons medium curry powder
2 teaspoons salt
4 bay leaves

⅛ teaspoon red pepper
2½ pounds lamb, cut in 1¼ inch cubes
Medium onions
Green peppers
Mushrooms

Mix together all ingredients except lamb, onions, green peppers and mushrooms. Marinate lamb in this mixture for 2 to 4 hours.

Cut onions in half horizontally and then cut in quarters. Cut peppers along section lines removing core, ribs and seeds. Remove stems from mushrooms.

Alternate on skewers lamb, onions, green peppers and mushrooms, cut to the same general size.

Grill shish kebabs over hot charcoal until nicely browned on all sides and pink in middle. Baste with the excess marinade or with a barbecue sauce.

Medieval dwelling decked out in resplendent modern colors.

All Purpose Barbecue Sauce

4	tablespoons chopped onion	3	tablespoons brown sugar
4	tablespoons olive oil	1	lemon, sliced thin
2	teaspoons dry mustard	2	teaspoons salt
4	tablespoons Worcestershire sauce	½	teaspoon black pepper
½	cup red wine vinegar	5	dashes hot pepper sauce
6	ounces tomato paste	4	tablespoons sherry
10	ounces beef bouillon		

Sauté onion in olive oil until brown and discard onion. Add rest of ingredients, except sherry and simmer a few minutes. Add sherry.

Makes about 3 cups.

This Barbecue Sauce is a flavorful, well-balanced sauce. It does not overpower as the bottled tomato based and hickory smoked versions generally do. This sauce is good on most barbecued meats.

Black Belt Barbecue Sauce

(For Pork)

3	garlic cloves, sliced	2	tablespoons Worcestershire sauce
1	stick margarine	1½	teaspoons dry mustard
2	cups cider vinegar	1	cup tomato ketchup
1	cup water	¾	teaspoon black pepper
⅓	cup sherry	3	dashes hot pepper sauce
2	tablespoons brown sugar	1½	teaspoons salt

Sauté garlic in margarine until limp. Add other ingredients and bring to boil; simmer for 10 minutes. If you prefer less vinegar flavor, simply add more margarine.

The recipe makes enough for 6 pounds raw meat.

This Barbecue Sauce with a significant amount of tomato ketchup is especially good with pork.

Maryland Basting Sauce

Use this sauce as a marinade and basting sauce for barbecued duck, chicken, spareribs or dove breasts wrapped in bacon.

1	clove garlic, sliced	2	teaspoons chili powder
3	tablespoons olive oil	1	teaspoon dry mustard
2	teaspoons freshly ground black pepper	1	teaspoon paprika
2	teaspoons salt	1	teaspoon ground cumin
1	teaspoon sugar	3	dashes hot sauce
2	bay leaves	¾	cup red wine vinegar

Simmer garlic in oil until limp. Add other ingredients and bring to boil and simmer about 5 minutes to combine well.

Makes about 1 cup.

Lamb Shoulder with Vinegar

(From the Italian Countryside)

2	pounds lamb shoulder	¼	teaspoon salt
2	tablespoons olive oil	¼	teaspoon coarsely ground black pepper
2	teaspoons finely chopped garlic	2	tablespoons minced parsley
⅓	cup red wine vinegar		

Have butcher cut lamb shoulder in 1 inch slices; then chop slices in 1½ to 2 inch chunks, leaving bone and fat in place.

Heat olive oil in a sauté pan over high heat until almost smoking. Add the lamb pieces in one layer and brown on all sides. Reduce heat to low, cover pan and simmer lamb slowly for 30 minutes. Turn meat occasionally. Sprinkle garlic in pan and continue cooking a couple of minutes until garlic is limp. Pour vinegar over lamb and scatter salt, pepper and parsley on top. Continue cooking a few minutes longer until flavors are blended.

You may add ½ to 1 teaspoon oregano with the salt and pepper if you like that flavor.

Pork Escallops with Orange Ginger Sauce

2 pounds boneless center cut pork chops or slices of pork loin (½ inch or thinner)

Salt and black pepper to taste

½ cup flour

4 tablespoons vegetable oil

1½ cups orange juice

3 tablespoons fresh gingerroot, scraped and minced

1½ tablespoons ground coriander

Pinch red pepper flakes

⅓ cup soy sauce

Season escallops with salt and pepper and dust with flour. Heat oil in a heavy skillet until very hot, but not smoking. Sear escallops until nicely browned on each side and just cooked through (3 to 4 minutes per side). Set aside and keep warm.

Pour oil out of skillet. Add orange juice to skillet and boil rapidly until reduced by one half (about 5 minutes). Add ginger, coriander, red pepper flakes and soy sauce. Boil rapidly and again reduce by nearly one-half (sauce should lightly coat the back of a spoon). Spoon sauce over escallops and serve at once.

Serves 6.

Preparing for a gala Barbecue:
O.C. Stodghill shovels coals under whole hogs.

Charcoal Broiled Pork Medallions

The Malleo, as well as the Collon Cura, Chimchuin and other Argentine rivers are among the premier trout streams of the world. There, rainbow and brown trout challenge lovers of fly fishing from many distant countries.

2½ pounds boneless pork loin
(cut in ½ inch slices – about 10 slices)

3 tablespoons olive oil

3 tablespoons lemon juice

4 tablespoons dry white wine

2 teaspoons dry mustard

1 tablespoon finely chopped garlic

½ teaspoon ground cumin

1 teaspoon rosemary, crumbled

1 teaspoon ground sage

½ teaspoon salt

½ teaspoon black pepper

2 tablespoons butter

Remove excess fat from pork medallions. Pound slices lightly with mallet until flattened and about ⅜ inches thick. Blend all ingredients except butter and put in a flat pan. Turn pork slices in marinade and cover pan for 30 minutes or so.

When ready to cook, put slices over hot charcoal or other grill. Cook 3 to 4 minutes on one side, then the other. Continue grilling until just cooked through (not more than 10 minutes in all). Heat marinade and swirl in the butter. Remove from heat. Return cooked pork slices to the marinade and cover for 3 to 4 minutes before serving.

Serves 5 to 6.

Asada at Hosteria San Huberto on the Malleo River, Argentina.

Pozole

(Kerry and Bailey Izard)

2	dried Guajillo chilies	1	large garlic clove, coarsely chopped
2	dried Ancho Pasilla chilies	½	cup coarsely chopped white onion
2	cups water	2	pounds boneless pork shoulder, trimmed and cut in 1 inch cubes
2	teaspoons oregano leaves, crumbled		
1½	teaspoons salt	3	cans white hominy, drained and rinsed (15 ounce)
¼	teaspoon black pepper		
¼	teaspoon cumin seed		

Stem and seed chiles. Put chilies and water in a small saucepan and simmer until softened (about 15 minutes). Replenish water as needed. Transfer chilies and water into a blender. Add oregano, salt, pepper, cumin seed, onion and garlic. Blend until smooth. In a 4 quart heavy pot put pork and chili purée and bring to a simmer. Add enough water to cover pork. Continue simmering, covered, for 1 hour. Skim off any fat. Add hominy and continue simmering for 30 minutes. Replenish water as needed. Taste for salt.

The Pozole should be accompanied by most of the following side dishes:

Fresh serrano or other mild peppers, coarsely chopped

Radishes, sliced

White onion, coarsely chopped

Fresh cilantro, chopped

Lime wedges

Warm corn or flour tortillas or tortilla chips

Serves 8 to 10.

Charcoal Broiled Spare Ribs

5	pounds pork spare ribs	½	teaspoon salt
½	cup cider vinegar (divided)	1½	teaspoons ground cumin (comino)
1	tablespoon celery salt	1½	teaspoons black pepper
½	teaspoon red pepper		

Rub spareribs with vinegar. Mix spices and rub into the meat, but do not coat.

Basting Sauce

⅓   stick butter

⅓   cup cider vinegar

⅓   cup water

Cook spare ribs slowly over medium hot charcoal. Baste occasionally. Meat should be done through and nicely browned (total cooking time about 45 minutes). If charcoal is hot, it is a good idea to cook ribs, bone side down, over indirect heat with grill lid down for the first 15 minutes or so.

Serves 6.

These ribs are quite spicy and may be served as is or you may accompany them with All Purpose Barbecue Sauce, p.167 or Black Belt Barbecue Sauce, p.167.

Baked Spare Ribs

5 pounds pork spare ribs, cut in serving-
   size pieces (smaller ribs are best)
6 tablespoons Worcestershire sauce
1 teaspoon ground sage
2 medium onions, sliced

Celery salt to taste
Lemon pepper to taste
Paprika to taste
Black pepper to taste

In a saucepan, cover spare ribs with water. Bring to a boil. After boiling a few minutes, skim off foam and add Worcestershire sauce, sage and onions. Continue cooking at a low boil until spare ribs are tender and cooked through - about 1 hour. Pour off water and onion and sprinkle ribs generously with celery salt, lemon pepper, paprika and a little black pepper.

Put spare ribs in a pan in a preheated 400 degree oven and bake until ribs are slightly crisp - about 20 minutes.

Baby back ribs work particularly well in this recipe.

Ribs are delicious as is, but they may be served with a mild barbecue sauce such as All Purpose Barbecue Sauce, p.167.

Serves 6.

Pigs and sausages in meat market, Buenos Aires.

Marinated Pork Tenderloin with Mustard Sauce

(Charcoal Broiled)

½	cup soy sauce		¼	cup brown sugar
½	cup bourbon		3	pork tenderloins each about 1 pound

In a ziploc bag, blend soy sauce, bourbon and brown sugar. Add tenderloins and marinate for several hours or overnight.

Grill the tenderloins over hot coals with the lid down until only a trace of pinkness remains in the center. Baste occasionally with the marinade. Try not to overcook. Serve with Mustard Sauce.

Mustard Sauce

¼	cup sour cream		1	tablespoon chopped scallions
¼	cup mayonnaise		2	teaspoons white wine vinegar
1½	teaspoons dry mustard			

Mix the sour cream, mayonnaise, mustard, scallions and vinegar. Let stand at room temperature for at least 4 hours or make a day ahead.

Serves 6.

Currant and Chutney Sauce

(For Pork)

¾	cup currant jelly		1	tablespoon brandy
½	cup finely chopped Indian chutney		½	teaspoon salt
1	teaspoon lemon juice			

In a small saucepan, heat currant jelly. Stir in other ingredients and continue heating until well blended.

Sausage, Cheese English Muffins

(Mary Samford)

1   pound country sausage (well seasoned, but not "hot")

2   jars Kraft Old English cheese spread (5 ounce) (may substitute 8 ounces coarsely grated, sharp Cheddar cheese)

¼   cup mild canned green chilies, finely chopped (fire roasted canned chilies are good)

6   English muffins

Crumble sausage in a frying pan and cook over medium heat until browned and done. Remove excess grease. Over low heat blend cheese spread with sausage and stir in green chilies. Split English muffins and spread each half with the sausage cheese mixture - about 1 heaping tablespoon per half muffin. Recipe makes about 12 halves.

At this point, you may wrap muffin halves in saran wrap and hold in refrigerator for one or two days or freeze for several months. When ready to serve, run muffins under the broiler about 6 inches from the heat source and broil until the sausage is bubbly and the edges of the muffins are browned (5 to 10 minutes).

Serves 6 to 8.

> These English Muffins, pulled from the freezer, can be the centerpieces of a wonderful country breakfast – perfect for a hunting or fishing trip.

Veal Scaloppine with Lemon and Capers

1   pound veal scaloppine

     Seasoned flour

3   tablespoons olive oil

1   tablespoon finely chopped garlic

3   tablespoons finely chopped onion

4   tablespoons capers

¼   cup dry white wine

3   tablespoons lemon juice

½   teaspoon basil

     Salt and black pepper to taste

Pound veal scaloppine between sheets of wax paper until a little more than ⅛ inch thick. Season flour with salt and pepper and lightly dust scaloppine. Heat olive oil in a sauté pan over medium heat and cook scaloppine in one layer until lightly browned, about 1 minute per side. Remove to a warm platter. Add garlic and onions to sauté pan and stir until they take on a little color. Add wine and scrape up brown bits in the pan. Simmer until reduced by one half. Add lemon juice, capers and basil. Stir all together, heat well, correct seasoning and pour over scallops. Serve at once.

Serves 4.

Veal with Fontina and Prosciutto

Unlike mature beef, there is little or no marbling in veal. Its only fat is on the outside of the carcass. Veal will therefore tend to be tough unless cooked long enough to be medium or at least medium rare. Curiously, the meat will begin to toughen again as it approaches well done. Veal that is braised or stewed and pounded veal scallops are exceptions to the foregoing considerations.

2 pounds veal cutlets (16 slices, ¼ inch thick)
16 thin slices prosciutto
⅓ cup flour
7-9 tablespoons butter (divided)

8 slices Fontina cheese, about ½ pound, cut in half
¾ cup dry sherry or Marsala
1¼ cups chicken broth
¼ cup chopped parsley

Place veal slices in a single layer on a flat surface. Top each with a slice of prosciutto. Place meat between 2 pieces of wax paper and pound to flatten slightly and to make prosciutto adhere to veal. Refrigerate at least 1 hour.

When ready to cook, dust both sides of meat lightly with flour. In large skillet melt 6 to 8 tablespoons butter over medium heat. Increase heat to medium high. Add meat, veal side down, a few pieces at a time, and sauté until brown, 5 to 7 minutes. Turn, sauté until prosciutto browns, 3 to 4 minutes. Transfer, prosciutto side up, to a large baking pan. Top each piece of meat with ½ slice cheese. Cover with wax paper.

Pour off drippings from skillet. Stir in sherry, cook over medium high heat 30 seconds, scraping up crusty bits in pan. Stir in broth. Bring to boil over high heat. Continue to boil until mixture is reduced by ½, about 5 minutes. Stir in 1 tablespoon butter and parsley, cook just until butter melts. Remove from heat, cover and keep warm.

Preheat broiler. Put pan with meat under the broiler until cheese melts, and meat is heated, about 2 minutes. Arrange meat on platter, pour sauce over it.

Serves 8.

Veal Mushroom Meatloaf

3 tablespoons butter

½ pound mushrooms, washed and chopped in ¼ inch pieces

¼ pound shiitake mushrooms, washed and chopped in ¼ inch pieces

2½ tablespoons finely chopped garlic

4 tablespoons finely chopped shallots (or onion)

2 pounds finely ground veal (top round or other inexpensive cut)

⅓ cup finely chopped spring onions (1 small bunch)

⅓ cup finely chopped parsley (lightly packed)

¼ cup bread crumbs (or 1½ slices white bread, crusts removed, and torn in dime size pieces)

1 egg

¼ cup whipping cream

1½ tablespoons Worcestershire sauce

2½ teaspoons thyme leaves

1 teaspoon salt

½ teaspoon black pepper

Melt butter in a sauté pan and add mushrooms, shiitake mushrooms, garlic and shallots. Over medium heat cook until mushrooms have given up most of their liquid, stirring frequently (about 10 minutes). Press mushrooms lightly and pour off any remaining liquid. Turn off heat and let cool.

To the veal, add the spring onions, parsley and bread crumbs. With hands mix ingredients well. Then mix the mushrooms with the veal.

In a separate bowl, beat egg and add cream, Worcestershire sauce, thyme, salt and pepper. Pour into veal-mushroom mixture and mix well with hands. Shape into a loaf; place in a loaf pan; and bake in a preheated 375 degree oven until juices are clear (35 to 40 minutes). This quantity fits in a 9 x 5 x 2⅝ inch loaf pan. Pour off juices and turn meatloaf out on a platter. Let settle for about 10 minutes before slicing.

Serve meatloaf with a rich brown sauce.

Serves 6 to 8.

For individual servings you can form meatloaf mixture into "hamburger steaks" and cook them in an iron skillet until nicely browned on both sides.

Vegetables

The freshest possible produce for the French table.

Vegetables

Previously, I nominated fried chicken as the South's signature dish, but the South truly excels in its treatment of vegetables. Cooks capitalize on the innate flavor of the vegetable and are not particularly fancy. In deference to this regional talent, there are more Southern recipes in this Section than elsewhere in this book.

Southern emphasis on vegetables is not accidental. Seasonal availability of truly fresh produce encourages a search for perfection. Corn and tomatoes, for instance, are entirely different when fresh from the field. Spinach, green beans and summer squash are also at their best when grown close to home. Recipes that profit from that homegrown flavor include Baked Corn and Tomatoes, p.189, Green Beans with Burnt Butter, p.187, and Sautéed Squash, p.207.

From an opposite perspective, fried vegetables dot the Southern table. Country Fried Potatoes, p.199, Fried Green Tomatoes, p.212, and French Fried Onion Rings, p.198, can each be memorable.

A recipe from Mary's family kitchen in Griffin, Georgia departs from the simplicity of some of these old favorites. Large carrots are parboiled until slightly soft and then hollowed out lengthwise. The removed part of the carrots is chopped, seasoned with mustard and spices and then heaped back in the carrots. Browned in a hot oven, Stuffed Carrots, p.188, are an unusual and very good dish for any fancy party.

Then there are recipes that are just more common in the South. Black-Eyed Pea Patties, p.181, Collard Greens, p.185, Squash Soufflé, p.208, and Jessie's Candied Sweet Potatoes, p.210, are probably less familiar in other parts of the country.

Late August, Helsinki, Finland.

Artichokes

4   artichokes   **½   teaspoon salt**

Trim and wash artichokes. Place artichokes in salted water to cover and simmer until leaf tips are tender; about 45 minutes. Test leaves for doneness. Depending on size, artichokes may take a little longer.

For much enhanced flavor, add to the cooking water:

¼   cup cider vinegar   **3   bay leaves**
1   lemon, sliced   **1   teaspoon whole black peppercorns**
1   medium onion, sliced

Serve artichokes hot with hollandaise sauce or melted butter seasoned with lemon juice; or cold with mayonnaise or vinaigrette dressing.

Serves 4.

Julia Child has said that she hates undercooked vegetables and that properly cooked vegetables are not "crunchy." I could not agree with her more.

Black-Eyed Pea Patties

1   cup dried black-eyed peas   **Flour for dusting**
1   teaspoon salt   **Bacon grease for frying**
1   teaspoon black pepper   **(any oil may be substituted)**

Simmer black-eyed peas in enough water to cover generously until well done (1 hour or more). Drain and slightly mash peas. Add salt and pepper.

Shape black-eyed peas into patties (about the size of sausage patties); sprinkle with flour on both sides; and fry in ⅛ inch hot bacon grease until well-browned on both sides.

This recipe is an excellent use for left-over black-eyed peas. Instead of sprinkling patties with flour, you may add 2 tablespoons flour to the black-eyed pea mixture.

Hollandaise Sauce

3	egg yolks	3	dashes cayenne pepper
1-1¼	sticks butter		Salt to taste
2	tablespoons lemon juice		

Cut stick of butter in about 8 pieces. In the top of a double boiler over simmering water, put egg yolks and one piece of butter. Stir vigorously with a wire whisk until butter is melted. Continue to whisk in butter one piece at a time. Sauce should begin to thicken when about two thirds of the butter is melted. If not thickening, or if the sauce is not thick enough, let the sauce get a little hotter. It may be necessary to continue whisking for 3 to 5 minutes after all of the butter has melted. After the sauce has thickened, gradually add the lemon juice with the rest of the butter. Add the cayenne and salt, if needed, at end. Last ¼ stick of butter is optional depending on how sauce is doing and how much you need.

The sauce may require little or no salt or as much as ½ teaspoon depending on the butter.

Regulating the heat is critical to the success of this recipe. Some cooks recommend keeping the water temperature below a simmer. I have better luck with the water simmering and keeping sauce from getting too hot by adding another piece of butter as soon as the previous one is melted.

Mouth watering Belgian white asparagus.

Baked Beans

(Ginny Tuttle)

1	pound navy beans	3	cloves garlic, minced
½	cup dark brown sugar	1	teaspoon salt
½	cup molasses or cane syrup	¼	pound salt pork, finely chopped
¾	cup ketchup	1	cup water
2	teaspoons dry mustard	¼	pound salt pork in one chunk
1	cup minced onion		

Select salt pork with streaks of lean rather than all fat. Soak beans overnight. Boil beans in fresh water to cover amply until skins pop when blown upon (about 15 minutes) In a bean pot or other oven proof container with a lid, mix brown sugar, molasses, ketchup, mustard, onion, garlic, salt, chopped salt pork and water. Then mix beans into the sauce. Slice ¼ pound lean salt pork partly through and fan out on top of beans. Bake covered in a 200 degree oven for 12 hours.

Quick Baked Beans

4	tablespoons molasses	4	teaspoons dry mustard
4	tablespoons chili sauce or ketchup	4	cans baked beans in tomato sauce (16 ounce)
2	tablespoons cider vinegar		
1	tablespoon Worcestershire sauce	2	medium onions, thinly sliced (about 1½ cups)
⅛	teaspoon cayenne pepper		

Blend together molasses and chili sauce. Stir in vinegar, Worcestershire sauce, cayenne pepper and dry mustard. Turn baked beans into a deep heat-proof casserole dish or heavy saucepan. Pour off some of excess liquid. Stir in molasses mixture and onion slices.

Bake casserole or saucepan in a preheated 350 degree oven until beans are heated through (30 to 45 minutes). Beans may be heated more quickly over medium heat on top of the stove if you are careful to stir often to prevent sticking.

Serves 8.

Caponata Siciliana

(From Rome)

1 medium eggplant, peeled and cut in ¼ inch dice	2 tablespoons white wine vinegar
4 tablespoons olive oil (divided)	2 teaspoons sugar
2-3 inside ribs celery, cut in 1 inch julienne strips (about ¾ cup)	½ teaspoon salt
	¼ teaspoon black pepper
1 medium onion, sliced thin and slices quartered (about 1 cup)	4 dashes cayenne pepper
	1-1½ tablespoons capers, minced
3 medium ripe tomatoes, peeled and seeded (about 1½ cups) (may use canned)	½ cup green (or black) olives, chopped

Sprinkle eggplant with salt and place in a colander weighted down with a plate. Let drain an hour or so and pat dry on paper towels (should be about 4 cups). In a sauté pan, cook eggplant slowly in 2 tablespoons olive oil for 20 minutes, stirring occasionally. Remove eggplant to paper towels.

Add 2 tablespoons olive oil to the pan and sauté celery and onion.

In a blender, fitted with the steel blade, purée tomatoes. When celery and onions are transparent, add tomatoes, vinegar, sugar, salt, pepper and cayenne pepper. Simmer for 10 minutes. Add capers, olives and reserved eggplant; cook 2 minutes. Correct seasoning.

Serve hot or at room temperature.

Pita chips go well with this dish.

Serves 8.

Collard Greens

2	bunches collard greens	2	inch chunk of salt pork
	Salt		Bacon grease (or ham bone)

Pick off leaves, discarding stems and tough outside leaves. Squeeze hands-full of greens and slice in ½ inch rounds. Put sliced greens in cold water; wash and scrub, tear and squeeze with hands to press out some of the strong juices. Drain greens, cover with fresh salted water and cook at a slow boil for a couple of hours with 2 inch chunk of salt pork. Add water as needed. Before serving (when cooked down) add about 1 tablespoon bacon grease per big serving and simmer a little longer. Instead of bacon grease, you can cook the collards with a ham bone.

Collards in White Wine

2	pounds smoked ham hocks, cut in medium pieces	2	teaspoons salt
1	cup chopped onion	2	cups dry white wine
1	tablespoon finely chopped garlic	2	pounds collards (weigh after cut up)
1	teaspoon hot sauce or to taste	2	tablespoons soy sauce

Wash and slice collard greens as described in preceding recipe for Collard Greens.

Put ham hocks, onion, garlic and hot sauce in an 8 quart pot with water to cover. Boil 5 minutes. Add salt, wine and collards and stir; then add soy sauce and stir again.

Cook collard greens covered over low heat 1½ to 2 hours stirring occasionally. Add more water if needed. (Do not, however, use too much water.)

Sautéed Eggplant

Eggplant should be diced or sliced, salted and let stand for at least ½ hour. This process will draw out some of the water and when later sautéed or fried, the eggplant will not absorb as much oil.

Young eggplant need not be peeled. If you do peel them, however, I find it easier to slice the eggplant first and then peel the slices.

1	medium eggplant	3-4	cloves garlic, minced
½	teaspoon salt	3	tablespoons shredded fresh parsley
3-4	tablespoons olive oil		

Peel eggplant and cut into ½ inch dice. Toss eggplant dice in a colander with the salt and let drain for 30 minutes. Dry the eggplant dice with a towel or paper towels. Heat the olive oil in a large sauté or frying pan over medium heat and spread the eggplant dice in the pan. Fry the eggplant, tossing frequently until it turns golden (4 to 5 minutes). Add more olive oil if needed. Sprinkle in the minced garlic and fry another couple of minutes. Lastly add the chopped parsley.

Serves 4.

California Style Green Beans

2	packages frozen French cut green beans*	½	teaspoon oregano
2	garlic cloves, finely chopped	¼	teaspoon black pepper
5	tablespoons olive oil	2	tablespoons chopped parsley
2-3	tomatoes, peeled		

Cut each tomato in 6 to 8 wedges and seed.

Cook beans in salted water according to package directions. Refresh beans under cold water. Put the garlic in a frying pan with the olive oil and sauté about 2 minutes. Add the beans and shake well. Add the tomatoes, oregano and pepper and shake well again. Leave on low heat until tomatoes are just heated through. Put in a hot serving dish and sprinkle with parsley.

Serves 6.

*You may substitute 1 pound fresh haricots vert or frenched green beans. In either case, cook beans in salted water until just tender and refresh under cold water.

Green Beans with Burnt Butter

2	pounds fresh green beans	Salt and black pepper to taste
1	stick butter	

Select small, fresh stringless green beans. Trim off stem ends and wash in cold water. Drop beans in enough rapidly boiling salted water to cover beans well. Reduce heat and simmer until beans are just tender.

Melt butter in a small saucepan and cook over low heat until frothy and nicely browned (5 to 10 minutes).

Pour butter over beans and season with salt and pepper.

Vegetable booth, Saturday market, Honfleur, France.

Stuffed Carrots

Thomas Jefferson spent time traveling in central France. He was particularly interested in the local cuisine and viniculture. Upon his return to Monticello, he tried to implement much of what he had learned. More than 200 years later, we followed in Jefferson's footsteps on a boat trip up the Rhône River.

8	large carrots	2	tablespoons finely chopped parsley
4	teaspoons prepared mustard	¼	teaspoon salt
3	tablespoons minced onion	⅛	teaspoon black pepper
2	teaspoons sugar	½	cup buttered bread crumbs

Boil carrots until almost done, 15 to 20 minutes. Remove skins. Hollow carrots out lengthwise similar to Indian canoes, but with thicker sides and bottoms.

Chop removed part of carrot very fine and combine with remaining ingredients except bread crumbs. (If chopped carrots are on the firm side, simmer in a little water until soft.) Heap mixture in carrots and top with buttered bread crumbs. Put stuffed carrots in an iron skillet or other oven proof pan with a little water and run into a preheated 450 degree oven until the carrots are heated, and the bread crumbs are lightly browned.

Serves 5 to 6.

French vegetable stalls.

Baked Corn and Tomatoes

6   ears sweet corn (approximate)
¼   cup chopped green bell pepper
¼   cup chopped onion
6   slices bacon

6   tomatoes, sliced (about 2½ cups)
Buttered bread crumbs (about 1 cup)
Salt and pepper to taste

Cut corn from cob. Mix bell pepper and onion with corn. Cook bacon, drain on absorbent paper and crumble. In a 1½ quart casserole dish alternate layers of the corn mixture and tomatoes, starting with corn and finishing with tomatoes. Lightly salt and pepper tomato layers. Top with generous layer of buttered bread crumbs which have been mixed with the crumbled bacon. Bake in a preheated 350 degree oven for about 1 hour. Casserole should be bubbly, and the crumbs lightly browned.

Like most good cooks, Muffet Corse gladly gave me her excellent recipe but omitted the quantities. You may therefore want to experiment with yours.

Creamed Corn

6   ears sweet corn
4   tablespoons butter
½   teaspoon salt

¼   teaspoon black pepper
½-1 cup milk

Select fresh, sweet corn with small to medium sized kernels. Husk corn and remove silk.

Melt butter in a large iron skillet and remove from heat. With a sharp knife cut corn from cobs into the skillet. The first vertical strokes with the knife should cut about half way through the kernels. The second time around slice all the way down to the cob. The idea is to cut the kernels approximately in half to release the milk from the corn. Season corn with salt and pepper.

Return the pan to medium heat and gradually stir in ½ to 1 cup milk. The quantity of milk varies with the amount of liquid released by the corn. You should end up with a creamy, cohesive dish.

Cover the pan and simmer until corn is tender (5 to 8 minutes). Stir occasionally. Add more milk, if needed.

Serves 6.

Dobe
(Okra and Tomatoes)

The name "dobe" has been used in the deep South for generations. It may have been derived from the French dish, "daube".

4	strips bacon	3	medium onions, sliced
4	tablespoons butter	4	ears sweet corn
8	medium tomatoes, peeled, seeded and quartered	10	ounces frozen cut okra
			Salt and black pepper to taste

Fry bacon until crisp; reserve. Melt butter in a saucepan and cook tomatoes and onions until almost done. Cut corn from the cob. Add corn and okra to the tomato mixture and cook another 10 minutes. Crumble bacon and add to dobe.

Dobe is generally served over boiled rice.

Freezes well.

Molly's Corn Fritters

4	tablespoons flour	2	tablespoons butter
1	teaspoon baking powder	2	eggs, beaten
1	teaspoon sugar	½	cup milk
½	teaspoon salt	2	cups freshly cut yellow corn
⅛	teaspoon black pepper		Canola or corn oil for frying

In a medium bowl mix flour, baking powder, sugar, salt and pepper. Melt butter and blend with flour mixture. Stir eggs and milk into the flour mixture and then add corn. Should make a medium batter.

Cook fritters (about 3 inches in diameter) over medium heat on a well-greased griddle or in an iron skillet until browned on both sides.

Serves 6.

Fried Grits

Cooked grits
Cornmeal

Bacon grease or vegetable oil

Pack warm grits in a highball glass or glasses and let chill thoroughly in the refrigerator. Tap glass on bottom to remove grits in a cylinder. Slice grits in ⅓ inch rounds and dredge both sides in cornmeal. Heat a thin coating of bacon grease (or vegetable oil) in an iron skillet and brown rounds on both sides. Remove to paper towels and drain.

Grits cakes are often served at breakfast with bacon, but can be used as a starch with any meal. Some people have even been know to put syrup on their grits cakes!

For those readers who are not fortunate enough to have Southern roots, grits may not be as common as they are here at home. Be that as it may, this recipe is perfect for leftover grits. You can, however, cook grits specifically for this purpose. Follow the directions on the box.

Morels

Morels
Salt

Butter
Black pepper

Cut morels in halves or quarters vertically and soak in lightly salted cold water for an hour or so. Pour off the water and rinse the morels under cold water to remove any remaining foreign matter.

Over medium low heat, melt a generous amount of butter in a sauté pan. Sauté the morels, stirring frequently, for 5 to 8 minutes. Season lightly with pepper; the rinse should provide enough salt. Serve the morels with red meat and red wine.

After sautéing the morels, you may whisk 1 to 2 tablespoons of flour into the butter remaining in the pan, then stir in enough milk to make a rich gravy. Correct the seasoning and pour over the morels.

Morels (Morchella Esculenta) are wild mushrooms with brownish, sponge like caps. They are great delicacies and grow in many parts of North America, including Georgia, Michigan and Montana. Jack Crockford, my hunting and fishing companion and good friend, remembers them as a child in Northern Michigan. While we were together in Southwest Montana, he struck the mother lode and harvested the largest quantity of morels that we had ever seen. Although morels occasionally appear in fine food stores, I am not aware of their being grown commercially.

About Onions

Members of the onion family take many forms-onions, garlic, shallots, leeks, chives. There are yellow onions, white onions and red onions. Some bear geographic names-Vidalia, Texas sweets, Walla Walla. Onions vary from the principal ingredient in a dish to a soupcon providing just a hint of flavor. Whatever their role, onions are a pivotal ingredient in a great many recipes.

Onions contain a network of very small cells separated by a fragile network of cellulose. Within these cells are various sulfur compounds. When the cells are broken down by cutting or mashing, the sulfur compounds combine setting off a chemical reaction that makes tears come to your eyes. These compounds also account for the strong onion taste in raw onions. The so called "sweet" onions have less sulfur content and therefore taste milder.

Cooking also breaks down the onion cells and releases the various sulfur compounds which then dissipate during cooking. For this reason a plain yellow onion which may be quite strong when tasted raw will taste just as good in a cooked dish as the more expensive mild onions.

A few comments on the various members of the onion family may be helpful.

Grading Vidalia onions.

Sweet yellow onions, formerly labeled Bermuda, are the most versatile. Vidalia, Texas Sweets and Walla Walla onions fall under this heading and are preferred when available. All of these onions are sweet and have a delicious onion flavor. They are perfect for salads. They are not as strong as some other members of the onion family, but will work in almost any recipe.

Vidalia is a town in Southeast Georgia. Onions grown in that region have a wonderful, sweet, mild flavor. Over the years, these special onions have gained wide recognition in the market under the Vidalia name. Because of the value of the name, onion growers further and further away from Vidalia began to label their onions "Vidalia". The Georgia General Assembly has, however, passed a law specifying the counties around Vidalia that can legally use its name. With regional pride, I vote for Vidalias as the best onions of the lot.

White onions have a more delicate texture and are the best choice when whole onions are used. Creamed onions are a good example.

Red onions tend to be a little stronger and are less desirable except when their color is a factor. On this basis, they are fine in many salads and as garnishes.

Spring onions are harvested while immature. With their tops, they are a good addition to a selection of vegetables served with a dip. Chopped, they go nicely in salads and are also used as a garnish, with gazpacho for example.

Shallots are close kin to onions. They have an intense onion flavor, but are not strong or bitter. Shallots are generally chopped and cooked as part of the seasoning in a sauce or other cooked dish. Béarnaise sauce is an example.

Garlic hardly needs an introduction. It is the backbone of much European cuisine-particularly Italian. Before use, garlic buds are dried, but should be firm, moist and unsprouted. Garlic is ordinarily sliced, minced or put through a garlic press. It is a natural with olive oil in cooking. It is also used in salad dressings.

A super-sized bulb known as Elephant Garlic is milder than its normal cousin, but tends to be more of a curiosity than a useful addition to the onion family.

Leeks are a large, mild member of the onion family. They may be braised, creamed or used as a base for soup. Vichyssoise is the leeks' most noble progeny.

Chives are a form of onion tops used as a seasoning. They accentuate their leek cousins in Vichyssoise.

Baked Onions

(In Foil)

6   medium yellow onions, preferably
      Vidalia or other sweet onions

6   teaspoons Worcestershire sauce

6   teaspoons butter

6   beef bouillon cubes

    Black pepper

Select 6 medium yellow onions of even shape. Peel onions and slice just enough off bottoms to make them sit evenly. Slice enough from top of onions to expose a large surface area. With a paring knife, carve out a depression in the top of each onion.

Place each onion on a square of aluminum foil large enough to fold over the onion. Pour 1 teaspoon Worcestershire sauce in each onion and top with 1 teaspoon butter and a bouillon cube. Sprinkle with black pepper. Fold the foil around each onion and seal. Place onions in a cookie pan and bake in a 350 degree preheated oven 45 minutes to 1 hour, or until onions are soft. Open the foil packages and spoon a little of the juice back into the onion cavities. Serve while hot.

Serves 6.

*Street vendors in a small town
along the Yangtze River in China.*

Vegetables 195

Charcoal Broiled Onions

6   medium onions, preferably Vidalia or
      other sweet onions

2-3 tablespoons butter

Worcestershire sauce

Salt

Black pepper

Select flat onions, preferably less than two inches thick. Cut in half horizontally and trim roots flat on bottom, leaving most of the skin intact. If onions are more than 2 inches thick, cut a slice or two from each cut surface and reserve for another use.

Place onions over a medium hot charcoal fire, root side down, and cook with the hood down until heated through. Shake a generous amount of Worcestershire sauce on each slice, top with several slivers of butter (about 1 teaspoon per slice) and sprinkle with salt and pepper. Continue grilling until onions are softened. Then turn onions and brown cut sides. Turn onions again and add a little more butter. Remove onions from grill and peel off dry outside skin. Serve onions with steak or other grilled meat.

Serves 6 to 8.

Charcoal Roasted Onion Halves

8   Vidalia (or other sweet) onions, peeled
      and cut in half horizontally

    Olive oil

    Balsamic vinegar

Salt

Coarsely ground black pepper

4   slices bacon, cut into 16 pieces

Place each onion half, cut side up, on a 10 inch square of heavy-duty foil. Drizzle with olive oil and vinegar. Sprinkle with salt and pepper. Top with a bacon piece. Fold foil around onions into neat packets.

Heat charcoal grill to medium hot. Place foil packets on grill; cook 20 to 30 minutes (if grill becomes too hot, move onions to a cooler section of the grill), until onions are tender and slightly charred. Let onions cool in packets for 15 minutes.

Remove foil, reserving juices; discard bacon. Put onions on a platter and serve warm or at room temperature. Drizzle the reserved juices over the tops of the onions.

Serves 8.

Onion Marmalade

(Abby Dunham)

1	stick butter	¾	cup sugar
3	pounds yellow onions	½	cup Jerez or balsamic vinegar
½	teaspoon salt	2	tablespoons grenadine
¼	teaspoon black pepper	¾	cup dry red wine

In a flame proof casserole dish or heavy saucepan, melt butter over low heat and simmer until it becomes golden (about 5 minutes). Peel onions and cut vertically in ¼ inch slices (should have about 2 quarts).

Add onions, salt, pepper and sugar to the butter. Simmer, covered, over low heat for 30 minutes. Stir occasionally with a wooden spoon. Add the vinegar, grenadine and red wine and continue simmering, covered, over low heat for 30 minutes more. Stir occasionally. Remove the lid and continue cooking over a low flame for 1 ½ to 2 hours until the marmalade begins to thicken like preserves (it will thicken more as it cools). Stir from time to time increasing the frequency as the marmalade cooks down.

Yields 3 to 3½ cups.

This recipe from Paris is especially good with duck. It may be served hot with meat or other fowl. Cold, or at room temperature, the marmalade marries well with pâtés, lamb and game.

Onion Patties

¾	cup flour	1	tablespoon cornmeal
2	teaspoons baking powder	¾	cup milk
1	tablespoon sugar	3	cups chopped yellow onion
¾	teaspoon salt		Vegetable oil for frying
¼	teaspoon black pepper		

Combine flour, baking powder, sugar, salt, pepper and cornmeal. Add milk and mix well. Stir in the onions. Cover the bottom of a heavy skillet with oil about ⅛ inch deep and heat until hot but not smoking. Drop small 3 inch mounds of batter into the hot oil and with a spatula flatten slightly. Fry patties about 5 minutes on each side, or until golden brown. Serve hot.

Serves 4.

French Fried Onion Rings

Most onion rings are coated with a batter of one sort or another and tend to be a little heavy. By contrast, these rings are light and crispy.

4	onions (medium size)	1	teaspoon salt
1	cup milk	1	teaspoon fine ground black pepper
1	cup flour		Vegetable oil for frying

Sweet yellow onions are desirable here. Once again, Vidalias are the best. Peel and slice onions in ⅛ inch slices. Separate slices carefully into rings. Soak onion rings in milk for ½ to 1 hour. The time that onions soak is not, however, critical.

Put flour, salt and pepper in brown paper bag. Shake onion rings in the bag, a handful at a time, until evenly coated with the seasoned flour.

Fry onion rings in hot vegetable oil (375 degrees) to cover generously (in small batches with the individual rings separated) until light brown (1½ to 2 minutes). Remove onions from oil, spread on paper towels, sprinkle with salt and keep warm. Serve promptly. A frying basket that fits a medium saucepan is very helpful in frying onion rings.

Creamed Leeks

4	large leeks (approximate)	½	cup chicken stock
3	tablespoons butter	⅛	teaspoon nutmeg
1½	teaspoons flour	¼	teaspoon salt
⅔	cup whipping cream	⅛	teaspoon white pepper

Cut leeks including the pale green parts in ½ inch slices. You should have about 3 cups of leeks. Separate slices into rings, cover with cold water and soak about 30 minutes. Drain leeks well.

In a large skillet over medium heat, melt butter until foam begins to subside. Add leeks, toss to coat with butter and cook for 2 to 3 minutes. Remove leeks and set aside.

Mix flour in cream; then gradually add cream and chicken stock to the pan in which the leeks were cooked. Over low heat, bring sauce to a boil and cook until sauce thickens, about 10 minutes. Stir occasionally. Add nutmeg, salt and white pepper. When sauce thickens, return leeks to pan and cook until leeks are cooked but not limp-about 5 minutes.

Country Fried Potatoes

4   medium baking potatoes, peeled and cut cross wise in ⅛ inch slices

2   medium yellow onions, cut in ⅛ inch slices

½   cup vegetable oil (approximate)
     Salt

If you have time, it is good to soak sliced potatoes in cold water for 30 minutes or so. Should have twice as much potatoes as onions.

Put enough oil in a large cast iron skillet to give a depth of about ⅛ inch. Heat oil until hot but not smoking. Dry potato slices and add to skillet. There should be about 2 layers of potatoes. Cook over medium heat until potatoes are brown on one side. Turn potatoes and add onions. Continue cooking and turning until potatoes are pretty well browned on both sides and onions are limp. Remove to paper towels as portions are done and sprinkle with salt.

Best to serve while still hot.

Serves 6 to 8.

Italian Potatoes

6   medium baking potatoes

½   cup fine bread crumbs (divided)

½   cup finely grated Parmesan cheese (divided)

2-3 large tomatoes, peeled and sliced

2   medium onions, thinly sliced

1½   teaspoons crumbled oregano leaves

1½   teaspoons salt

¼   teaspoon black pepper

¾   cup olive oil

Peel and cut potatoes in thin wedges. Mix bread crumbs and cheese. Reserve a small amount of bread crumbs and cheese to sprinkle on potatoes. Rinse potatoes and while wet mix with the remaining bread crumbs and cheese.

Coat the interior of a 9 x 13 inch baking dish with olive oil and spread potatoes in the dish. Sprinkle with reserved bread crumbs and cheese. Cover potatoes with a full layer of tomatoes; sprinkle tomatoes with salt and pepper; and top with a full layer of onions. Drizzle onion layer generously with the olive oil. Bake uncovered in a 350 degree preheated oven about 1¼ hours or until onions are browned, but dish retains some crunchiness.

Serves 8 to 10.

Hashed Brown Potatoes

3-4	medium size russet (baking) potatoes		Salt and black pepper to taste
½	cup chopped onion	3	tablespoons butter (divided)
4	tablespoons vegetable oil (divided)		

Making good hashed browns is not an easy trick, and there are many theories on how to proceed. The accompanying recipe works well for a couple of reasons. Chilling the potatoes in the refrigerator makes the starch crystallize. This chemical reaction keeps the potatoes from getting too mushy. Second, plenty of oil and butter are necessary ingredients to the crispy brown exterior that is essential to good hashed browns. Some will remember short order cooks using an old baking powder can to chop cold potatoes on their greasy griddles!

Bring a large pot of salted water to a boil and add the potatoes. Bring the water back to a boil and cook until potatoes are tender. (They should be barely cooked through the center if you test by cutting one in half.) Time varies with size of potatoes and amount of water, but 15 to 20 minutes should suffice. Pour off cooking water and cover potatoes with cold water. When potatoes are cool, peel and store in the refrigerator for at least 1 hour.

When ready to cook the hashed browns, slice the potatoes in ⅜ inch slices and chop medium fine (should have somewhat more than 3 cups). Combine and mix the potatoes, onion, 1 tablespoon vegetable oil and a generous amount of salt and pepper.

In a 9 to 10 inch skillet, melt 2 tablespoons oil and 2 tablespoons butter. When the foam subsides, add the potato mixture and mash down with a spatula. Cook over medium heat until well browned on the bottom (about 10 minutes). Put a large plate over the pan and invert the pan sliding the potato cake out onto the plate. Use the spatula to help. Melt the remaining 1 tablespoon oil and 1 tablespoon butter in the pan. Slide the potato cake back on the uncooked side and continue cooking until browned (about 10 minutes). Slide onto a serving platter and serve while hot.

Serves 4.

Lyonnaise Potatoes

6-8 white new potatoes (or 3 to 4 baking potatoes), peeled and sliced ¼ inch thick

2-3 medium onions, peeled and sliced ¼ inch thick

¾ stick butter

Ground nutmeg

Salt

Black pepper

2 beef bouillon cubes

½ cup half-and-half

Sizes of potatoes and onions vary, but you should have 2 to 3 times as much potato as onion.

In a sauté pan over medium heat melt butter and sauté onions until they take on a slight yellow hue. Try to keep slices more or less intact.

Butter an ovenproof casserole dish or cast iron skillet. Alternate single layers of potatoes and onions ending with potatoes. Sprinkle each layer generously with salt and pepper and a few dashes of nutmeg. Preferably, use 3 or 5 layers with total depth not over 3 inches. Dissolve bouillon cubes in one cup of hot water and pour in enough liquid to half cover the potatoes and onions.

Bake in a preheated 400 degree oven 30 to 45 minutes until potatoes are done and partly browned on top. Most of the liquid should have been absorbed. About 10 minutes before the potatoes are done pour the half-and-half over them. If you do not have, or want to use, half-and-half, this recipe is quite good without it.

The presence of beef bouillon in the foregoing recipe may be unusual, but these potatoes go well with red meat or other hearty fare.

Potato-onion combinations have been associated with the Lyon District of France, but no consistent recipe has emerged. The name Lyonnaise Potatoes is therefore applied to a variety of potato-onion-cheese baked dishes.

Pappas Fritos
(Argentina)

4	medium baking potatoes	½	cup finely chopped parsley
3-4	cups vegetable oil	¼-½	cup olive oil
6	cloves garlic, finely chopped		Salt

Peel potatoes and cut lengthwise as for French fries. Heat vegetable oil in a medium saucepan until a thin slice of potato sizzles and turns brown in about 1 minute (375 degrees). Drop potatoes in the oil in relatively small batches so that they are not crowded in the pan and cook potatoes until golden brown. Use a frying basket, if available.

Meanwhile heat an iron skillet and pour in olive oil - enough to make a thin layer in the bottom of the skillet. While potatoes are draining, add the garlic and parsley to the hot skillet. Add the drained potatoes and toss and stir until well coated with the garlic-parsley mixture. Salt to taste and serve immediately.

Potato Pancakes

3	medium potatoes	¼	teaspoon black pepper
⅔	medium onion	2	tablespoons flour (or matzo meal)
2	eggs		Vegetable oil for frying
¾	teaspoon salt		

Peel and coarsely grate potatoes (about 2 cups) and onion (about ½ cup). Mix potatoes and onions. Beat eggs well and stir into potato and onion mixture. Add salt, pepper and flour and blend.

Heat ⅛ inch vegetable oil in an iron skillet. Spoon in about 1 heaping tablespoon of batter and flatten with a spatula until thin. Cook until nicely browned on one side. Turn and brown the other side.

Potato pancakes are good served with sour cream and apple sauce as accompaniments.

Ratatouille

(Vegetable Casserole Provençale)

4   tablespoons olive oil (approximate) (divided)

2   medium onions, cut in medium slices

1   green bell pepper, seeded, cored and cut in medium slices

½   medium eggplant, peeled and cut in medium slices

3   yellow squash or small zucchini, cut in medium slices

3   medium tomatoes (not too ripe), cut in medium slices

1   tablespoon basil or to taste

    Salt and black pepper to taste

1   large clove garlic, thinly sliced

My good friend, Jack Burton, makes an excellent Ratatouille in a cast iron skillet. Putting a little olive oil in the skillet, he sautés the same ingredients, adding them in the order listed above. He substitutes canned tomatoes for the fresh.

Put 1½ tablespoons olive oil in the bottom of a flame proof casserole dish. Then alternate layers of onions, green pepper, eggplant, squash and tomatoes in that order. Sprinkle every other layer with basil, salt, pepper and a little garlic and drizzle with a little olive oil.

Cover casserole and cook over low heat 30 to 35 minutes until vegetables are done. Stir contents slightly from time to time. To reduce liquid cook uncovered for last 10 minutes or so.

Onions drying in a field near Vidalia, Georgia.

About Rice

The three common types of rice are white rice, brown rice and wild rice. Various forms of flavored rices are marketed, but they are not included in this cookbook.

Brown rice is the current rage because of its superior nutritional value. Unless rice is a large part of your diet, this quality does not seem overly significant. Nevertheless, unless the entrée suggests white or wild, brown rice is fine.

When rice is intended as a foil to distinctively flavored dishes, white rice is much the better choice. White rice should be used with curries, Creole dishes, gravies and the like.

Wild rice is not actually a member of the rice family, but a wild aquatic grass, common in Michigan and Minnesota. It has a pronounced flavor contrasted with the foil that white rice provides. It is designed to stand up to other dishes. As an example, wild rice is excellent with wild game.

Interesting customers at French village market.

Boiled Rice

1 cup long grain white rice	1 teaspoon salt
2½ quarts water	

In a 4 quart saucepan bring water to a rolling boil. Stir in salt and slowly sprinkle in rice. Continue at a slow boil until rice reaches desired degree of tenderness, about 15 minutes. Err on the undercooked side.

Drain rice in a colander and rinse well under cold water. Set colander over the saucepan with an inch or so of water. Bring water to a boil, put top on colander, and let rice steam until rice is well heated, at least 10 minutes. It does no harm to steam somewhat longer. Fluff rice with a fork and serve.

Boiling rice in a quantity of water is the old fashioned method. If you are careful to test rice for doneness during the last few minutes of cooking, it is fool proof. This method produces very fluffy, never soggy, rice. Recipes that cook away all the water are somewhat more "iffy". The same is true of rice cookers.

Green Rice

(Riz Verte)

3 tablespoons butter	½ cup milk
1 clove garlic, mashed	2 cups grated Gruyère cheese
1 medium onion, minced	2 cups cooked white rice
2 eggs	2 cups chopped parsley
½ cup olive oil	Salt and black pepper to taste

Melt the butter and sauté garlic and onion until they take on a little color. In a medium bowl beat eggs lightly and add olive oil, milk and cheese. Then add the butter, garlic and onions. Combine with rice, parsley, salt and pepper. Pour mixture into a buttered baking dish and bake in a preheated 375 degree oven for 45 minutes.

Serves 8

Spinach with Olive Oil and Garlic

4	tablespoons olive oil	1	pound fresh spinach, washed and coarse stems removed
2	large garlic cloves, thinly sliced		Salt and black pepper to taste

In a wok or sauté pan, heat olive oil and cook garlic until it takes on a little color.

Rinse spinach, shake off excess water and while still wet, heap into the wok or sauté pan. Turn spinach with a wooden spoon until all of spinach is wilted. Continue cooking for 3 or 4 minutes, stirring occasionally. Spinach should keep its green color and not be over cooked.

Season with salt and pepper to taste.

Serves 4.

Baked Acorn Squash

3	acorn squash	6	tablespoons sherry
5	tablespoons butter		Salt to taste
3	teaspoons brown sugar		Paprika to taste

Slice each squash in half horizontally and add to each half: about ¾ tablespoon butter, ½ teaspoon brown sugar and 1 tablespoon sherry. Sprinkle with salt and paprika to taste.

Put squash in a baking pan with a little water. Bake in a preheated 375 degree oven for 45 minutes or until squash is tender. Baste occasionally. During last few minutes, if squash halves look dry, add a little more butter and sherry.

Serves 6.

Sautéed Squash

6-8 medium yellow squash, cut in medium slices

1-2 medium onions, cut in medium slices

3 tablespoons bacon grease

¼ teaspoon salt

¼ teaspoon black pepper

You should have about ¼ as much onion as squash. Melt bacon grease in sauté pan and add squash. Cook over medium heat, stirring occasionally, for 5 to 10 minutes until squash is limp. Add onion slices, salt and pepper. Cook another 5 to 10 minutes stirring occasionally. Then add ½ cup water, cover and simmer for ½ hour or so. Remove cover and continue cooking until most of water evaporates. Correct seasoning and serve.

Stuffed Yellow Summer Squash

8 medium yellow summer squash

½ cup finely chopped onion

3 tablespoons butter

Salt and black pepper to taste

Buttered bread crumbs

In a large saucepan cover squash with water and bring to a boil. Simmer until squash just begins to get soft (about 8 minutes). Remove squash from pot and refresh under cold water. Cut a long oval from the top of each squash and with a spoon, scoop out the insides being careful not to tear the squash shells. Pour off excess liquid and finely chop the removed tops and insides of the squash. Melt 2 tablespoons butter in a skillet and sauté onions until just limp. Stir in the chopped squash and season with salt and pepper.

Mound the squash onion mixture back into the squash shells and cover with a layer of buttered bread crumbs. Put squash in a pan with a little water and bake in a preheated 450 degree oven until the bread crumbs are nicely browned (about 10 minutes).

Serves 4 to 6.

Squash Soufflé

2½	pounds yellow squash	½	cup flour
1½	cups chopped onion	¼	teaspoon black pepper
2½	teaspoons salt (divided)	1	pint milk
½	stick butter	3	eggs, separated

Wash, trim and scrape spots from squash. If squash are large, cut in chunks. Place squash and onions in a boiler with enough water to cover and add 1½ teaspoons salt. Cook until squash is tender (15 to 25 minutes depending on size of squash). Remove squash from heat and drain well. Let cool a few minutes.

In a small saucepan, melt butter and make a cream sauce with flour, remainder of salt, pepper and milk. Whisk the milk in slowly and continue stirring over low heat until the sauce is quite thick. Remove from heat and stir in egg yolks. Let cool.

Mash drained squash and onion well. Pour off any excess liquid. Add cream sauce to squash mixture and combine. Beat egg whites until stiff but not dry. Fold egg whites into squash mixture.

Butter and flour a 2 quart casserole dish. Pour squash mixture into casserole. Bake uncovered in a preheated 350 degree oven for about 1 hour. The soufflé should be brown on top and the inside only slightly runny.

Serve immediately.

Serves 6.

If you like a cheese flavor, sprinkle top of soufflé with a cup of grated Parmesan or sharp Cheddar cheese before baking.

Spaghetti alla Puttanesca

4	large cloves garlic, finely chopped	¼	teaspoon crushed red pepper
4-5	tablespoons olive oil (divided)	1½	teaspoons oregano leaves
1	pound tomatoes, peeled and coarsely chopped (2 large tomatoes)	10	ounces spaghetti or vermicelli
4	tablespoons capers	2	ounces anchovies, finely chopped
½	cup sliced black olives	½	cup finely chopped parsley
			Salt to taste

Puttanesca roughly translates as in the style of ladies of the night. The origin of this designation is not known.

In 2 tablespoons olive oil, sauté garlic until it takes on a little color. Add the tomatoes, capers, olives, red pepper and oregano and simmer over medium heat for about 10 minutes.

Add the rest of the oil, anchovies, parsley and salt, if necessary. Stir and heat. Cook the pasta in boiling salted water. Drain. Mix sauce with hot pasta and serve immediately.

Serves 6.

Spaghetti Squash

2	medium spaghetti squash	Salt and black pepper to taste
½	stick butter	

Spaghetti squash are somewhat unusual, but you will find them in the markets from time to time. Keep your eye out for them.

Split spaghetti squash in half lengthwise; remove seeds; place squash cut side down on a cookie pan; and bake at 350 degrees until squash is tender (45 to 60 minutes). Remove squash from oven and with a table fork working in a lengthwise direction, strip out the squash pulp. It will look just like fine pasta. Melt butter and pour over squash. Season with salt and pepper.

Serves 8.

Instead of being served with butter, spaghetti squash is very good with any mild pasta sauce. Sauce Alfredo is particularly good.

Jessie's Candied Sweet Potatoes

4-5 medium sweet potatoes	¼ teaspoon ground nutmeg
¾ cup orange juice	1 teaspoon vanilla extract
¾ cup Karo light corn syrup	1 lemon, sliced
⅓ stick margarine	1 orange, sliced
¼ teaspoon ground allspice	

Peel sweet potatoes and cut into uneven chunks each large enough for 2 bites, or so. Instead of chunks, you may use ½ inch slices cut in half or you may cut the potatoes like steak fries. Just suit your fancy.

Melt margarine in a cast iron skillet and add sweet potatoes, orange juice, syrup, spices and lemon and orange slices. Cook over medium low heat, stirring occasionally, until potatoes are done and sauce has thickened (about 1 hour). Then run skillet under broiler about 6 inches from the heat for 10 minutes or so until exposed corners of potatoes and fruit are browned. Do not use salt or pepper in this dish.

Instead of cooking sweet potatoes on top of the stove, you may bake this dish in a preheated 375 degree oven for 1½ to 2 hours until potatoes are well done, browned on corners and the syrup has darkened. The first method, however, seems to make the dish thicker and the flavors a little more intense.

Vegetable salesmen monitor (facing page)
and haggle (above) on market day in Viviers, France.

Fried Green Tomatoes

Gravy may sound strange with fried green tomatoes, but you will be surprised what a great combination the two make.

Growing up, our favorite Sunday breakfast was pan fried center cut ham, fried green tomatoes, grits and gravy. To cook this breakfast, first brown the ham in a cast iron skillet with a little oil; then fry tomatoes in the same pan. Finally make the gravy and put it in a sauceboat to be poured on the ham, tomatoes and grits as suits the diner's taste.

3-4 large green tomatoes
Flour for dredging
Salt and black pepper to taste

Vegetable oil for frying
Milk for gravy

Tomatoes that are just showing signs of pink are ideal. Slice tomatoes about ½ inch thick. Do not peel. Season flour well with salt and pepper. Dredge tomato slices in seasoned flour until well coated on each side.

Generously cover the bottom of a cast iron skillet with oil and place over medium heat. When the oil is hot, but not smoking, put in one layer of tomatoes. Cook until nicely browned on one side; then turn and brown the other side. Keep tomatoes warm while others cook. Add more oil as needed.

You may substitute cornmeal for the flour.

When all of the tomatoes are cooked, add to the pan 3 to 4 tablespoons of the flour used for dredging and stir until the flour takes on a little color. Scrape up and stir in all of the browned scraps of tomatoes. Gradually whisk in 1 to 2 cups of milk until the gravy is nicely thickened. Season with salt and black pepper.

Serves 6 to 8.

Savory Broiled Tomatoes

4	medium tomatoes (not too ripe)	8	teaspoons brown sugar
	Salt	½	cup finely chopped onion
	Black pepper	½	cup buttered bread crumbs

Slice tomatoes in half horizontally. Scoop out tops of halves to make slightly concave surfaces.

On each half sprinkle the following ingredients in the order listed:

	Salt and black pepper to taste	2	tablespoons onion
1	teaspoon brown sugar	1	tablespoon buttered bread crumbs

Put tomatoes in a cookie pan and bake in a preheated 450 degree oven until crumbs are browned and tomatoes are cooked through but still firm (12 to 15 minutes).

Serves 4.

Jessie's Stewed Tomatoes

½	stick butter	1½	tablespoons cider vinegar
1	can peeled tomatoes (28 ounce)	¼	teaspoon ground allspice
¾	cup chopped onion	1	teaspoon vanilla extract
2	teaspoons sugar		Salt and black pepper to taste

In an iron skillet melt butter, add tomatoes and simmer until slightly thickened (30 minutes or so); then add onions. Continue cooking until quite thick (15 to 30 minutes). Add sugar, vinegar, allspice, vanilla and salt and pepper to taste. Simmer another 10 minutes.

Tortilla
(Spanish Potato Omelet)

The Spanish eat tortillas at every meal. Tortillas are available at tapas bars as a hot or warm vegetable. They are wonderful cold at picnics.

For a family vacation, we rented a 16th century palatchio (Spanish for an estate with a tower, chapel and other features) in the lovely village of Treceno, Spain. It once belonged to an ancestor of the prominent Atlanta architect, Henry Jova, who beautifully restored it to its former elegance. Home cooked Spanish meals – a remarkable stew involving beans, pork, various innards and turnip greens; fried fresh sardines; and tortillas – were highlights of our visit.

4	cups baking potatoes, peeled and cut in ½ inch dice (5-6 potatoes)
1	cup onion, chopped in ¼ inch dice (one medium onion)
¾	cup chopped red or green bell pepper (one small bell pepper)
¾	cup olive oil
1	teaspoon salt
5	large eggs
¼	teaspoon black pepper

Sprinkle salt on diced potatoes. Heat oil in a 9 inch skillet. Add potatoes. Oil should almost cover potatoes. Cook over medium heat until potatoes are three quarters done (about 10 minutes) (do not brown). Stir occasionally. Add onion and bell pepper, mix and continue cooking. When potatoes are soft (about 5 minutes longer), mash a few with spatula to make the mixture bind better.

Beat eggs in a large bowl and add the black pepper. With a slotted spoon, remove potato mixture from the skillet draining off most of the oil. Add potato mixture to the eggs and mix well.

Pour off all but 2 tablespoons of oil from the skillet, and over low heat, add egg-potato mixture. Shake pan to encourage eggs to run under sides of the tortilla. When mixture is well set, cover pan with a plate, invert pan and leave the tortilla on the plate. Slide the tortilla back into pan on the uncooked side and continue cooking over low heat. Shape edges of tortilla to vertical. Remove when tortilla is done through; do not brown. Serve hot or at room temperature. Keeps well in the refrigerator for a snack or picnic.

Serves 6 to 8.

Cooking the ubiquitous Spanish tortilla.

Breads

Bread lady, happy and well suited to her calling, Cabezon de la Sal, Spain.

Breads

An accomplished baker, I am not. Again from the South, however, some excellent cornmeal recipes are included as well as a camp bread, Bannock, p.220.

Among the Southern favorites are Cornbread, p.221, Cornmeal Lace Cakes, p.222, and Spoon Bread, p.224. Although each is dependent on cornmeal, they run the gamit from substantial cornbread to soufflé-like spoon bread. Another cornmeal dish, Mrs. Ralph Izard's Awendaw, combines cornmeal and grits. Although attributed to one of my Charleston ancestors, I have no idea how it survived to modern times.

Pancakes, p.224, Waffles, p.223, and Hush Puppies, p.223, are included because the recipes taste just right to me.

Sidewalk booth, Paris street market.

Mrs. Ralph Izard's "Awendaw"

1½ cups cooked grits	1½ cups milk
1 heaping tablespoon butter	¾ cup cornmeal
3 eggs	½ teaspoon salt

While grits are still hot, add butter and gradually add milk. Beat eggs until very light and stir into grits mixture. Then stir in the cornmeal and salt. The batter should be the consistency of thick custard. Pour the batter into a deep greased pan and bake in a 375 degree preheated oven about 1 hour.

This dish will take the place of spoon bread and is much more fool proof.

Serves 6 to 8.

Origin of the term "Awendaw" is unknown. I have several ancestors named Ralph (pronounced "Rafe" in the old English manner) Izard who lived in the low country of South Carolina in the eighteenth and early nineteenth centuries. There is, however, no reference to this recipe in our family archives.

Baking Powder Biscuits
(Molly's Recipe)

2 cups flour	4 tablespoons shortening (Crisco was the old standby)
4 teaspoons baking powder	¾ cup milk
½ teaspoon salt	

Sift together flour, baking powder and salt. Add shortening and mix in thoroughly with a fork.

Add liquid slowly to make a soft dough. On a floured board roll or pat dough out with hands to ¼ inch thickness. Handle dough as little as possible. Cut with biscuit cutter first dipped in flour (preferably about 1½ to 2 inches in diameter).

Put biscuits on a greased pan and bake 10 to 12 minutes in a preheated 450 degree oven. Biscuits should be nicely browned on top.

Makes 14.

Bannock

(Camp Bread)

Bannock was a staple for outdoorsmen who camped out while working in the woods. I was introduced to it by Jack Crocford, the distinguished director of the Georgia Game and Fish Department.

4	cups flour	6	tablespoons butter
4	teaspoons baking powder	2½-3	cups milk (or 1½ cups evaporated milk and 1 cup water)
1	teaspoon salt		

Mix flour, baking powder and salt. Melt butter in an iron skillet and stir butter into milk and then combine milk with flour mixture. You should have a fairly thick dough. Turn dough into the iron skillet that has been coated with the melted butter and level the surface. Dough should be about 1½ inches thick. Bake in preheated 375 degree oven for about 40 minutes or until nicely browned.

Serves 4 to 6.

You may substitute self rising flour for the flour and baking powder.

Bran Muffins

2	cups boiling water	1	quart buttermilk
14	ounces all bran cereal (1 box) (divided)	5	cups flour
2	sticks butter	5	teaspoons baking soda
3	cups sugar	1	tablespoon salt
4	eggs	3	cups raisins

In a large bowl, pour 2 cups of boiling water over 2 cups of all bran cereal and set aside. Cream butter and sugar in a mixer. Add eggs, one at a time, beating well each time. Add buttermilk and beat.

Add buttermilk mixture to the scalded bran. Sift flour, soda and salt and stir into the mixture along with the remaining 4 cups of all bran cereal.

Batter can then be cooked, refrigerated or frozen.

To cook: bake in a 375 degree preheated oven in greased muffin tins (any size) for 15 to 20 minutes.

Buttered Bread Crumbs

½ stick butter	1 cup dry bread crumbs

Put butter and crumbs in a small sauté pan or skillet. Over low heat melt butter while stirring to combine with crumbs. When well combined, the crumbs are ready to use. You may seal buttered crumbs in a ziploc bag and keep them indefinitely in the freezer.

Buttered crumbs make a more uniform crust than "dotting crumbs with butter". Moreover, the process is easier.

Cornbread

½ cup flour	1½ cups medium ground cornmeal (preferably white)
1 tablespoon baking powder	4 tablespoons butter
2 teaspoons sugar	2 eggs
¾ teaspoon salt	1 cup milk (approximate)

In a small bowl, combine flour, baking powder, sugar and salt. Then mix in the cornmeal.

Preheat oven to 425 degrees and heat a 9 inch cast iron skillet until sizzling hot. Remove skillet from oven and melt butter in it coating sides of skillet.

In a larger bowl, beat eggs with a fork and combine with milk. Pour in the excess butter from the skillet and stir. Add the dry ingredients to the milk mixture and combine quickly without stirring too much. You should have a thick batter that still pours. Pour batter into the sizzling skillet, smooth over the top and bake uncovered in the preheated 425 degree oven until nicely browned and cooked through (about 25 minutes).

Remove from oven and let stand 10 minutes or so before slicing in wedges.

Serves 6.

You may substitute bacon drippings for the butter to give a country flavor.

Cornmeal Lace Cakes

(Jesse's Fried Bread)

1	cup finely ground cornmeal (unbolted)	Water
1	teaspoon salt (scant)	Corn oil for frying

This bread recipe comes from southwest Georgia. The late Jesse Oliver, an experienced railroad cook, made these cakes to perfection. The quotations are from him. Jesse's name is mentioned in connection with several other wonderful south Georgia recipes.

Jesse had many wise sayings. Among my favorites: "A woman doesn't realize that when she pulls her man down off the bank, she is down in the mud with him."

Mix meal and salt. Stir in enough cold tap water to make it "kinda soupy" (slightly more than 1 cup of water). Set mixture aside for an hour or so, until it "tightens up."

When ready to cook, stir in enough water to make it "kinda soupy" again. The batter should be thinner than pancake batter and will not "tighten up" again.

Put a liberal amount of corn oil on a griddle over medium heat. Spoon batter onto hot griddle making cakes about 3 inches in diameter. Brown on one side, flip and brown on other side.

As Jesse said "the secret is the heat." If the heat is right, the grease will bubble up through the cakes making numerous small holes and the cakes will be brittle when slightly cooled. If the griddle is not hot enough the cakes will be doughy like a pancake; if the griddle is too hot the batter will splatter and fly apart. Trial and error is the only way to find the correct heat setting. You should add oil frequently.

Line a cookie pan with paper towels. Put lace cakes on the towels and keep warm in the oven.

Serves 6.

Cornbread Stuffing

4½	cups cornbread, crumbled	¼	teaspoon black pepper
¾	cup stale bread, crumbled	½	teaspoon powdered sage
1½	cups coarsely chopped celery (some leaves, if available)	½	teaspoon thyme leaves
¾	cup coarsely chopped onion	½	stick butter
¾	teaspoon salt	1	cup chicken stock (approximate)

Mix together all ingredients except butter and chicken stock. Melt butter, add to dressing and then moisten dressing with the chicken stock (the amount of stock will vary slightly to achieve the desired consistency). Dressing should be on the dry side.

Stuff bird about ¾ full.

Hush Puppies

1	cup regular grind, unbolted cornmeal	⅓	teaspoon black pepper
½	cup flour	⅓	cup finely chopped onion
1½	teaspoons baking powder	1	egg
1	teaspoon sugar	¾	cup milk
1	teaspoon salt		Vegetable oil for frying

In a bowl mix first 6 ingredients. Then add onion and mix well. Beat egg with a fork, add milk and then combine with dry ingredients. You should have a thick, tacky batter.

Have vegetable oil at least 2 inches deep in a saucepan. Heat over medium heat to about 350 degrees. Drop batter in oil by the heaping teaspoon. Do not crowd. Hush puppies will float to surface and should be nicely browned in about 1½ minutes.

Drain hush puppies on paper towels and keep warm.

For Variety Add

½ cup green bell pepper, finely chopped or

⅓ teaspoon thyme leaves or ⅓ teaspoon celery salt

Note: instead of cornmeal and flour mixture, try all fine or medium ground cornmeal.

Hush puppies are a must with fried fish!

Hush puppy batter is quite tacky, and it is often difficult to drop teaspoon quantities into the hot grease. If you dip your teaspoon in ice water, however, the batter will not stick.

Waffles

3	cups flour	4	eggs, separated
1½	teaspoons salt	3	cups milk (maybe more)
1½	tablespoons baking powder	8	tablespoons shortening (butter or margarine), melted
2	tablespoons sugar		

Sift dry ingredients together. Beat egg whites until stiff and set aside. Beat yolks; stir in milk and then butter or margarine (melted and slightly cooled). Combine dry ingredients with egg mixture, but do not beat. Fold egg whites into the batter. Cook batter on lightly greased waffle iron to desired degree of browness.

Serve with maple syrup and melted butter.

Serves 6 to 8.

Pancakes

The imperfection of early batches of pancakes is undoubtedly the origin of the expression – "The first pancakes is for the chilluns".

1	egg	2	teaspoons baking powder
1	cup milk	½	teaspoon salt
4	tablespoons butter, melted	2	tablespoons sugar
1	cup flour		

Beat egg and stir in milk and melted butter. Sift dry ingredients together and add to the liquids. Stir as little as possible to combine. Do not be afraid to leave lots of small lumps.

Cook pancakes on lightly greased, medium hot griddle. Adjust heat so that bubbles come through pancakes in about a minute and cakes are nicely browned on one side. Turn and brown the other side.

Getting the heat under the griddle just right is important. It will probably be necessary to make slight adjustments after the first batch or so.

Serves 4 to 6.

Spoon Bread

This recipe for spoon bread was made famous by the Hotel Roanoke, the old Norfolk and Western Railroad Hotel.

1½	cups fine ground white cornmeal	4	tablespoons butter
1½	teaspoons salt	5	eggs
1	teaspoon sugar	2	cups milk
1½	cups water	1	tablespoon baking powder

Mix cornmeal, salt and sugar. Bring water to boil and stir into the cornmeal mixture. Melt the butter and mix with the cornmeal mixture. Beat eggs well, add milk and combine well. Stir eggs and milk into the cornmeal mixture; then add baking powder and mix well.

Pour mixture into a greased baking dish and bake in a preheated 350 to 375 degree oven 30 to 40 minutes until mixture is set and slightly browned on top. Serve immediately.

It is important to mix ingredients in the order noted. This recipe fits nicely in a 9 x 13 inch baking pan.

Serves 10.

Can make ½ the recipe in 7½ inch round casserole dish.

Popovers

3	large eggs		1	cup flour
1	cup milk		¼	teaspoon salt
1	tablespoon butter, melted		2	tablespoons butter, cut in 6 pieces

Popovers are cooked in a special pan designed for that purpose. Oil the popover pan. Preheat the oven to 400 degrees and put rack in the middle of the oven. Preheat the popover pan for 2 minutes.

Beat eggs with a fork and stir in milk and 1 tablespoon butter. Add flour and salt and blend. Batter should be at room temperature and like thin pancake batter.

Put 1 piece of butter in each cup of the popover pan and put pan back in the oven until contents are bubbly (about 1 minute). Fill cups ½ full of batter and bake 20 minutes at 400 degrees. Reduce heat to 325 degrees and bake 10 to 15 minutes longer. Serve immediately. Popovers will rise well above tops of cups and should be brown and crisp on top. Times may vary slightly depending on your oven.

Makes 6.

Holiday popovers, baked by our daughter, Sarah I. Pariseau.

Desserts

Municipal Market, Oxford, England.

Desserts

From my previous references to favorites, one can tell that desserts are not at the top of my list. As is the case throughout this cookbook, however, I have tried to put together an unusual collection of particularly good recipes.

Among the best are foreign entries: Raspberry Roulade, p.239 (English); Tiramisu, p.240 (Italian), and Baked Papaya Mauna Kea, p.236 (Hawaiian—at least not part of continental U.S.).

Once again two recipes from my wife's family, Apple Dumplings, p.229, and Charlotte Russe, p.230, are outstanding as are Key Lime Pie, p.234, Lemon Soufflé, p.235, and Strawberry Sorbet, p.240.

Egyptian father and son tending a fruit stand, Alexandria, Egypt.

Apple Dumplings
(Sallie Porter)

For Pastry Dough

2   cups flour (scant)

2   tablespoons Crisco
    (or other vegetable shortening)

Ice water

Quickly mix flour, Crisco and enough ice water to make pastry dough. Roll dough out thin on floured board. Cut in 8 rounds (about 6 inches in diameter).

Filling

3   cups cooking apples, peeled, cored and
    coarsely chopped

1½ sticks butter (divided) (or a little more)

1½ cups sugar (divided)

1   teaspoon ground nutmeg (approximate)

Sprinkle apples with ½ cup sugar. Put ⅓ cup apples on each pastry round. Fold dumplings in half and pinch edges together. Spread 1 tablespoon softened butter on top of each dumpling and sprinkle with 1 tablespoon sugar and a generous amount of nutmeg. Place dumplings in a greased iron frying pan and bake in preheated 450 degree oven about 35 minutes until brown. Baste dumplings with pan juices after 15 minutes; check after 30 minutes.

Sauce

1-1½ cups water

½   cup sugar

½   stick butter

Remove dumplings from the pan; add about 1 to 1½ cups water, ½ cup sugar and ½ stick butter. Over low heat, simmer sugar mixture until it thickens into a syrup. Pour syrup over dumplings. Let dumplings cool until crisp, but not cold, and serve. Whipped cream or vanilla ice cream are nice additions.

Serves 8.

Charlotte Russe

4	eggs, separated		Dash of vanilla
6	tablespoons sugar (heaping)	1	quart whipping cream
3	ounces bourbon	2	tablespoons gelatin
1½	ounces Meyers dark rum		(2 envelopes, ¼ ounce each)
1½	ounces brandy	½	cup hot water
	Pinch of salt	2	(3 ounce) packages ladyfingers

In three separate bowls:

(small bowl) beat egg yolks; stir in sugar until blended; mix in liquors; and add salt and vanilla.

(medium bowl) whip cream until stiff.

(large bowl) beat egg whites until stiff.

Dissolve gelatin in ½ cup hot water and add to egg yolk mixture. Line serving bowl(s) with ladyfingers split in half lengthwise (reserving 8 halves for the top).

Gently fold contents of 3 bowls together, adding egg whites last. Pour mixture into lined bowl(s) and top with ladyfinger halves.

Cool in the refrigerator for several hours. Keeps well for several days.

Serves 8.

Municipal Market, Oxford, England.

Aunt Jean's Famous Cheesecake

	Butter	1¾	cups sugar
	Graham cracker crumbs	1	lemon, juice and grated rind
2	pounds cream cheese, room temperature	1	teaspoon vanilla
4	eggs		

Butter a soufflé dish and sprinkle heavily with graham cracker crumbs. (Or spray non-stick cooking spray on individual small paper liners; put the liners in small muffin tins; and sprinkle them with graham cracker crumbs.)

Beat cream cheese, eggs, sugar, lemon and vanilla until smooth. Pour the mixture into the soufflé dish or small cups. Set dish or muffin tin in a pan with ½ inch boiling water. Bake 1½ to 2 hours in a preheated 325 degree oven until firm. (About 25 to 30 minutes for the small muffin tin.) Turn off oven and leave dish or tin in the oven for 20 minutes. Remove dish or tin from oven and put on rack to cool. Refrigerate overnight, then invert on a plate.

Sauce

1	jar fruit jam (10 ounce) (apricot or cherry are good choices)	¼	cup water
		3	tablespoons cognac, brandy or kirsch
¼	cup sugar		

Combine all ingredients in a saucepan and cook over low heat until sugar is melted.

This delicious recipe originates with my sister-in-law, Jean Owen Izard.

Serves 8.

Quick Chocolate Mousse

(Leila Cheatham)

6 ounces semisweet chocolate bits or baking chocolate

½ cup hot strong coffee (instant coffee works well)

2 eggs, lightly beaten

2 tablespoons dark rum

1 cup whipping cream

Extra cream to taste

Chocolate, slivered for garnish

In a food processor fitted with the steel blade, blend the chocolate bits and hot coffee until the chocolate is melted. If you use the baking chocolate, cut the chocolate in small pieces. Add the eggs and rum and continue blending until smooth. Transfer the chocolate mixture to a serving bowl.

In a chilled bowl, whip the cream until it forms soft peaks. Then fold the cream into the chocolate mixture (reserving a little cream for the garnish). Chill 2 hours or more.

Garnish the Mousse with more whipped cream and/or slivered chocolate.

Serves 4.

Cocoons

½ pound butter or margarine

3 heaping tablespoons powdered sugar

2½ cups sifted flour

1 cup finely chopped pecans

2 teaspoons vanilla

Powdered sugar for dusting

Cream butter or margarine and sugar. Add flour, pecans and vanilla, using hands to mix. Continuing with hands, shape dough into individual rolls about ½ inch in diameter and 2 inches long. Rolls should be curved slightly.

Bake rolls on slightly greased pan in preheated 250 degree oven for 25 to 30 minutes. When cool, roll cocoons in powdered sugar.

Curried Fruit

6   tart, well flavored, apples or an equivalent amount of peaches, apricots or pineapple or best of all, a combination of these fruits

2   tablespoons butter
½   cup brown sugar
2   teaspoons mild curry power
½   teaspoon salt

Peel, core and slice fruit. In shallow baking dish over low heat, melt butter and stir in brown sugar, curry powder and salt. Continue cooking until all of the sugar is melted. Add fruit and stir until fruit is well coated with sugar mixture. Put baking dish in preheated 300 degree oven and bake until fruit is tender, about 35 minutes.

Serves 4.

Curried Fruit is a good choice for dessert with a casual dinner or can be served with dinner. Curried Fruit is particularly good with ham or lamb dishes.

Joan's Fruit Pie

(Blackberries, Blueberries, Sliced Apples, Peaches or Other Fruit)

¾   cup flour
1½-2   cups sugar (divided)
2   teaspoons baking powder
  Dash of salt
¾   cup milk

¾   stick butter or margarine, melted
2   cups fruit, blackberries, blueberries, sliced apples, peaches or other fruit
2   tablespoons lemon juice

Combine flour, 1 cup sugar, baking powder, salt and milk. Pour mixture into a slightly greased deep dish, about 8 inches in diameter. Pour butter on top. Do not stir. Mix fruit with ½ to 1 cup of sugar depending on sweetness of fruit and the lemon juice. Pour the fruit into the middle of the dish. Do not stir. Bake 1 hour in a preheated 350 degree oven.

Miraculously, the crust will rise to the top and brown.

Vanilla ice cream goes wonderfully with this pie.

Serves 6.

Key Lime Pie

This recipe is the original one for key lime pie. Some modern versions involve egg whites, lime zest and other refinements; but this old favorite is hard to beat.

3   eggs yolks (small)

14   ounces sweetened condensed milk (Carnation works well)

½   cup fresh lime juice (preferably from key limes)*

½   teaspoon cornstarch

1   (7 inch) graham cracker pie shell

Whisk egg yolks until light; combine with milk, lime juice and cornstarch; and continue whisking briskly until light in color.

Pour mixture into the pie shell. Bake about 20 minutes in a preheated 300 degree oven. When done, the center of the pie should be set but still quivery. Cool pie on a rack; then refrigerate.

To fill a 9 to 10 inch pie shell, use 4 egg yolks and 50% more of the other ingredients.

*Eight or ten key limes or three or four large limes will make ½ cup of juice.

You may decorate pie with thin lime slices or top with a layer of sweetened whipped cream, but the pie is delicious as is.

Homemade Graham Cracker Pie Shell

1⅓ cups graham cracker crumbs

½   teaspoon ground cinnamon

4   tablespoons sugar

2   tablespoons melted butter

Mix all ingredients well. Spray pie tin with non-stick cooking spray. Press crumb mixture into bottom and sides of pie tin. Recipe will make a 9 to 10 inch pie shell.

It is much easier and almost as good to purchase a graham cracker pie shell.

Serves 6.

Lemon Soufflé with Wine Sauce

1 tablespoon gelatin (1 – ¼ ounce envelope)	1 tablespoon grated lemon rind
¼ cup cold water	1¼ cups sugar
5 eggs, separated	1 cup whipping cream
¾ cup lemon juice (about 5 lemons)	

Dissolve gelatin in ¼ cup cold water. Beat egg yolks with a fork. Combine egg yolks, lemon juice, lemon rind and sugar in a saucepan. Cook over low heat, stirring constantly, until mixture is slightly thickened, about 8 minutes. Remove from heat and stir in the gelatin mixture until completely dissolved. Chill about 20 minutes.

Beat egg whites until stiff; fold into the lemon mixture. Whip cream; fold into the lemon mixture. Pour mixture into a 2 quart soufflé dish and chill at least 4 hours. This dessert may be made the day before, but perhaps looses a little of its airiness.

Serve with wine sauce.

Serves 8.

Wine Sauce

½ cup sugar

1¼ tablespoons cornstarch

½ cup water

3 tablespoons lemon juice

2 teaspoons grated lemon rind

2 tablespoons butter

¼ cup dry white wine

Our son, Bailey, in the Georgia mountains.

In a small saucepan, mix sugar and cornstarch; add water, lemon juice and lemon rind. Stir until smooth. Add butter. Bring sauce to a boil, lower heat and cook until thickened (happens very quickly). Remove sauce from heat. Stir in wine. Chill. Stir before serving.

Baked Papaya Mauna Kea

An outstanding dessert from the old Rockefeller resort on Hawaii and entirely reliable as long as the papayas are ripe.

1½ cups cottage cheese
1½ cups cream cheese
1½ teaspoons mild curry powder
1 tablespoon cinnamon sugar
  (1 teaspoon ground cinnamon to
  2 tablespoons sugar)
2 tablespoons chopped chutney

3 tablespoons white Sultana raisins
½ cup canned thinly sliced water chestnuts
4 ripe papayas, cut in half lengthwise and seeded
Melted butter
Cinnamon sugar

In a food processor fitted with the steel blade, blend until smooth: cottage cheese, cream cheese, curry powder, 1 tablespoon cinnamon sugar and chopped chutney. Add raisins and water chestnuts and mix with a spoon.

Pile mixture into papaya halves until slightly rounded. Brush with melted butter and sprinkle liberally with cinnamon sugar. Bake in a preheated 400 degree oven for 20 to 30 minutes until nicely browned.

Serves 8.

Orangelena

1 quart orange sherbet
3-4 medium oranges

¼ cup Cointreau or to taste

This recipe is at its best with orange water ice, but orange sherbet will do. Peel oranges and cut them into sections. Put the sherbet in a serving dish and arrange the orange sections on the sherbet in a circular pattern. Pour the Cointreau over the dessert.

Carefully slicing and arranging the orange sections makes a very pretty presentation and a delicious summer dessert.

Serves 6.

Peach Ice Cream

3 cups well ripened peaches, peeled and sliced

1½ cups sugar (divided)

3 cups half-and-half*

1 teaspoon vanilla extract

Pinch of salt

Mash peaches to a thick pulp with a potato masher or other suitable implement. Stir in ¾ cup sugar. Set aside.

Mix half-and-half, the other ¾ cup sugar, vanilla and salt. Put the half-and-half mixture in an ice cream freezer and process until cream begins to freeze. Then add the peach mixture and continue processing until ice cream reaches proper consistency. Remove dasher, pack the ice cream and hold in ice cream freezer until ready to serve or store in the freezer. Keeps well for several weeks.

May garnish ice cream with a few slices of ripe peaches.

*For a richer ice cream, use 1½ cups half-and-half and 1½ cups whipping cream.

Do not forget to use rock salt with the ice if using an old fashioned ice cream freezer.

Makes 2 quarts.

Georgia peaches!

Pears with Ginger

(Consie Mallory)

6 pears, cut in half vertically
2 teaspoons ground ginger
½ cup dark brown sugar

½ cup water
½ stick butter or margarine
Yogurt or sour cream for garnish

Peel and core pear halves. Put ginger, brown sugar, water and butter or margarine in a frying pan and combine over medium heat. Add pear halves, cover pan and poach for about 30 minutes or bake in preheated 350 degree oven for about 45 minutes (until pears are tender). Serve pears warm with yogurt or sour cream.

Serves 6.

Poached Pears in Orange Sauce

8 pears (firm)
1¼ cups orange juice
½ teaspoon grated lemon rind
½ teaspoon ground cinnamon
3 whole cloves

8 orange slices about ⅛ inch thick with the orange pulp removed
1½ teaspoons cornstarch
¼ cup cold water

Peel pears; remove core, leaving stem end intact. In a small saucepan combine orange juice, lemon rind, cinnamon and cloves and bring to a boil.

Select a saucepan that will just hold the pears standing up. Place pears in the pan, stem ends up and pour sauce over them. Put an orange slice around the neck of each pear. Cover the pan and simmer over the low heat 15 to 20 minutes until pears are tender. Remove pears with a slotted spoon.

Combine cornstarch and water and pour into sauce. Cook over low heat, stirring constantly, until sauce thickens. Pour sauce over pears.

Serves 8.

Raspberry Roulade

(Gloria - Maiden's Green, England)

1   pint raspberries   **Dark brown sugar**

½   pint whipping cream

Spread raspberries about 2 berries deep in a shallow baking dish. Whip cream until it holds stiff peaks. Spread cream over berries about ½ inch thick. Cover cream with a layer of brown sugar about ¼ inch thick. Run baking dish under a preheated broiler about 4 inches from the heat for 60 seconds or just a little longer. Brown sugar should fuse without melting much of the whipped cream. Serve at once.

This recipe also works with strawberries and probably other fruit.

Raspberry Roulade is an elegant dessert from an old family home in England.

Strawberries Romanoff

(S.S. Constitution, 1955)

1 pint fresh strawberries	1½ ounces kirsch
1½ cups almond macaroons	1½ ounces Cointreau
1 pint vanilla ice cream	1½ ounces sherry
1 cup whipping cream	1½ ounces brandy

Wash and clean strawberries. Cut large ones in halves. Sprinkle strawberries with Kirsch.

Dry macaroons in 200 degree oven until crisp (macaroons will dry more quickly if you break them in large pieces). Crumble macaroons coarsely. Whip cream until it holds stiff peaks.

Put ice cream in a silver bowl. At the table, or just before ready to serve, break ice cream into spoon size pieces; add strawberries and crumbled macaroons. Toss lightly to mix and at the same time sprinkle ice cream mixture with the other 3 liqueurs. Spoon whipped cream on top and serve.

This desert is almost equally delicious without the whipped cream if you want to save a few calories, a few cents or a little trouble, as the case may be.

Serves 6.

Strawberry Sorbet

This sweet, but tart, strawberry sorbet is delicious, quite different from the cloying sweetness of many water ices.

1	quart fresh ripe strawberries	2	cups water
1½	cups sugar	½	cup lemon juice

Wash, cap and slice strawberries (makes nearly a quart of berries). Cover berries with sugar and let stand for a few minutes. Put strawberries and sugar in a food processor fitted with the steel blade. Puree. Mix with water and lemon juice.

Freeze in an ice cream freezer until firm; remove dasher; pack sorbet and hold in ice cream freezer packed in ice until ready to serve or store in the freezer. Keeps well for several weeks.

For a slightly different effect, you may add 2 teaspoons finely grated lemon peel with the lemon juice.

Tiramisu

1	pound mascarpone cheese	1½	cups very weak coffee (can make with 1 teaspoon instant coffee)
8	eggs, separated (divided)		
½	cup sugar	½	cup brandy
½	cup very strong coffee (can make with 2 teaspoons instant coffee)		About 30 ladyfingers
			Cocoa powder (unsweetened)

Beat the mascarpone with a wooden spoon until soft and creamy. Beat 6 egg yolks in a separate bowl until fluffy and pale yellow. Add sugar to yolks a little at a time and continue beating until smooth. Add to mascarpone. Slowly stir in strong coffee. Beat 8 egg whites separately until stiff. Fold into cheese mixture.

Pour weak coffee and brandy into a bowl. Dip the ladyfingers one at a time and arrange in layer in a shallow bowl. Cover with about 1½ inches of the cheese mixture and sprinkle generously with cocoa. Repeat layers until all ingredients are gone. (Top layer should be ladyfingers.)

Chill at least 1 hour.

If the ladyfingers absorb all of the coffee brandy mixture, make another batch.

Serves 8 to 10.

Wine Gelatin

1	cup fresh lemon juice (and lemon rinds)	4	tablespoons gelatin (4 envelopes, ¼ ounce each)
6	cups water (divided)	1	cup sherry
1-1½	cups sugar (divided)		Few drops red food coloring
¼	teaspoon salt		Sweetened whipped cream for garnish

In a small saucepan bring rinds of about 3 lemons and 3 cups of water to a boil.

Stir in 1 cup sugar and salt.

Soak gelatin in 3 cups cold water. Combine hot and cold mixtures and stir in lemon juice and sherry. Add up to ½ cup more sugar depending on the sweetness of the sherry. Add a few drops red food coloring. Mix thoroughly and pour into a cold, wet mold. Put in refrigerator for 2 hours or more until firm.

Unmold and garnish with whipped cream.

Wine gelatin is the perfect gift for anyone who is not feeling well. It has a refreshing taste and is easily digested.

Hard Sauce

1	cup granulated sugar	Ground nutmeg
⅔	stick butter (approximate)	

With a fork mash the sugar into the butter until combined into a firm paste. Use as much butter as you can without making the sauce greasy. Shape sauce into a mound and sprinkle generously with ground nutmeg.

Most recipes for Hard Sauce specify powdered sugar, but I much prefer the coarse texture of granulated sugar.

Hard Sauce is an essential accompaniment for mincemeat pie and plum pudding.

Beverages

*Intent artisan trimming slices
of coconut meat, Istanbul, Turkey.*

Beverages

This volume is not intended as a bartender's guide, but this section includes a few especially good concoctions. On the soft side are a spicy Tomato Juice Cocktail, p.248, and an interesting Dr. Justice's Party Punch, p.246.

On the hard side, a couple of drinks are worth mention. Planters' Punch, p.247, is much more complex than its usual treatment and avoids excessive sweetness inherent in most Planters' and Rum punches. The recipe originated in the 60's at French Leave, a popular resort on Eleuthra, Bahamas. The bartender declined to part with his secret, but after watching him in action for a couple of nights, I came up with the recipe. Not only does the drink contain the usual ingredients but also brandy, bourbon and a second type of rum. Unfortunately, French Leave burned to the ground a year or two after our visit.

On the more traditional side, Eggnog, p.245, handed down from Mary's grandmother, is a rich version of this holiday treat. Our Christmas is never complete without a silver bowl full.

Hawaiian night at a South Georgia hunting lodge.

Eggnog

6	eggs, separated
⅔	cup powdered sugar
1	cup bourbon
½	cup brandy

½	cup medium rum
1½	pints whipping cream
1	cup milk
	Ground nutmeg

Homemade eggnog makes a festive holiday dessert.

Beat egg yolks until yellow. While continuing to beat slowly add sugar and continue until well blended. Stir in bourbon, brandy and rum. Set aside, preferably for 1 to 3 hours.

Beat cream until thick and combine with egg yolk mixture. Stir in milk. Beat egg whites until they hold stiff peaks. Gently fold into the eggnog.

Pour eggnog into a silver bowl. Sprinkle a little nutmeg on top of the bowl or put a dash on each serving.

For eggnog thick enough to eat with a spoon, omit the milk. If you prefer your eggnog less fluffy, omit the egg whites.

Irish Coffee

Irish whiskey	**Sugar**
Strong coffee	**Lemon juice**
Whipped cream	

Rub rims of wine glasses with lemon juice. Dip glasses in a saucer of granulated sugar. Twirl rims of glasses through flame (sterno or candle) until sugar crystallizes on the rims.

Put a jigger (about 1½ ounces) of whiskey in each glass. Fill with hot coffee to about 1 inch from rim. Top each glass with 2 tablespoons of whipped cream and serve.

Pisco Sour

(Chile)

Pisco Sour is a Chilean drink that is popular in Argentina. It packs a wallop!

1½	ounces Pisco	1	egg white
1	tablespoon sugar (or more)		Lime slices for garnish
1	tablespoon lime juice		

Mix all ingredients except lime slices in a blender or stir vigorously with ice in a bar glass. Serve over ice with a slice of lime.

A nice touch is to sugar coat the rim of the glass. The drink is also good without the egg white.

Dr. Justice's Party Punch

Slowly mix

1	quart good bourbon	3	ounces honey

Add

4	ounces rum	1	teaspoon angostura bitters
8	ounces lemon juice	1	tablespoon cherry juice

Pour mixture into a punch bowl with a big chunk of ice and add:

1	quart club soda	1	quart ginger ale

I am not partial to punch, but this recipe is very good.

Pepper Sherry for Bloody Marys

1 cup of dry sherry	2 small hot red peppers

In a small saucepan bring sherry to a boil. Add red peppers. Boil 5 minutes. Bottle the pepper sherry.

Pepper Sherry is distinctive in Bloody Marys in place of hot sauce.

Planters' Punch

(French Leave, Eleuthra)

1 ounce orange juice	1½ ounces medium rum
1 ounce pineapple juice	½ ounce brandy
¾ ounce lemon juice	½ ounce Myers's dark rum
1½ teaspoons grenadine	Dash of bourbon
2 dashes angostura bitters	

Mix foregoing ingredients in a pitcher or 16 ounce glass. Have the following ingredients to add to the drinks:

Club soda

Freshly ground nutmeg to taste

Slices of orange and maraschino cherries for garnish

Fill 2 highball glasses with ice, then pour in punch about 1 inch from the top. Mix well. Add 1 ounce or so of club soda to each glass and stir. Top with a splash of dark rum. Sprinkle with freshly ground nutmeg and garnish with slice of orange and a maraschino cherry.

Makes 2 to 3 drinks.

St. Cecelia Society Punch

The historic Debutante Ball in Charleston, South Carolina given by the Saint Cecelia Society is the origin of this potent beverage.

10   limes or 6 lemons
1   ripe pineapple
1   fifth cognac
1   pint dark rum
1   quart strong green tea

1   fifth peach brandy
3   cups sugar
4   quarts dry champagne
2   quarts club soda

Thinly slice the limes or lemons; peel and slice the ripe pineapple. Marinate the fruit overnight in a covered crock with a fifth of cognac. At noon on the day of serving, add the dark rum, the green tea, the peach brandy and the sugar. Blend these well. At the last minute, stir in the dry champagne and club soda. Pour over a block of ice in a large punch bowl. Serve in chilled punch cups.

Tomato Juice Cocktail

For an interesting touch and a slightly different taste, garnish each drink with a pickled banana pepper, pepperoncini or okra. Then stir in a couple of teaspoons of the pickle juice (from the bar in the old Bozeman Hotel in Montana).

4   cups tomato juice
4   tablespoons lemon juice
2   tablespoons Worcestershire sauce
1   tablespoon horseradish

2   teaspoons celery salt
1   teaspoon salt
4   dashes hot sauce
1/8   teaspoon black pepper

Mix all ingredients well and chill.

If the tomato juice cocktail is made the night before, you may add 4 thin slices of onion separated into rings, the tops of 2 or 3 ribs of celery including the leaves and 2 bay leaves. These additions make an unusual and refreshing cocktail. Remove vegetables before serving.

This tomato juice cocktail may also be used as the base for Bloody Marys.

Setting up an apple cider and calvados display, Honfleur, France.

Lye Soap

This recipe for lye soap slipped into my cookbook because I wanted to include the wonderful picture of Rosa Oliver boiling the soap. It typifies a bygone era.

In the rural Southeast at the dawn of the twentieth century, homemade lye soap was the standby for clothes washing and other household uses. Here, Rosa Oliver is making lye soap. She put a gallon or so of left over cooking grease in an iron pot over an open fire. To this she added a can of lye and gradually stirred in 2 to 3 gallons of water as the soap cooked down. When it became syrupy, she put the soap aside to cool. The soap was then cut into squares and laid out on an old burlap sack to dry.

Making lye soap,
Rosa Oliver remembers.

250

Index

C

Q

R

S

A Traveler's Table

John Izard

Please send me _____ copies of **A Traveler's Table** @ $24.95 each _____

Florida residents add 7% state tax @ $ 1.75 each _____

Shipping and handling @ $ 4.95 each _____

TOTAL _____

(PLEASE PRINT)

Name _____

Address _____

City _____ State _____ Zip _____

Make checks payable to: A Traveler's Table *and Mail to:* Mrs. Robert H. Pariseau, 807 S. Newport Ave., Tampa, FL 33606

For credit card orders, call 1-800-727-1034 or order online at wimmerco.com

---

A Traveler's Table

John Izard

Please send me _____ copies of **A Traveler's Table** @ $24.95 each _____

Florida residents add 7% state tax @ $ 1.75 each _____

Shipping and handling @ $ 4.95 each _____

TOTAL _____

(PLEASE PRINT)

Name _____

Address _____

City _____ State _____ Zip _____

Make checks payable to: A Traveler's Table *and Mail to:* Mrs. Robert H. Pariseau, 807 S. Newport Ave., Tampa, FL 33606

For credit card orders, call 1-800-727-1034 or order online at wimmerco.com